Childminder's
Handbook

Also available from Continuum

Childminder's Guide to Play and Activities – Allison Lee

Good Practice in the Early Years 2nd Edition – Janet Kay

Observing Children and Young People 4th Edition – Carole Sharman,
    Wendy Cross and Diana Vennis

Protecting Children 2nd Edition – Janet Kay

Childminder's Handbook

Allison Lee

continuum

Continuum International Publishing Group

The Tower Building
11 York Road
London
SE1 7NX

80 Maiden Lane, Suite 704
New York,
NY 10038

www.continuumbooks.com

The websites and information addresses featured in this book were up-to-date at the time of writing, however, it is suggested that individuals preview the sites to ensure the content remains accurate and appropriate.

Allison Lee has asserted her right under the Copyright, Designs and Patents Act, 1988, to be identified as Author of this work

British Library Cataloguing-in-Publication Data
A catalogue record for this book is available from the British Library.
ISBN: 0–8264–9024–7 (paperback)

Library of Congress Cataloging-in-Publication Data
A catalog record for this book is available from the Library of Congress.

Typeset by Ben Cracknell Studios | www.benstudios.co.uk
Printed and bound in Great Britain by The Cromwell Press, Trowbridge, Wiltshire

Contents

Introduction

With pressure on people to return to work after having families, more and more parents are looking to childminders and nannies to provide the care they require for their children. Home-based childcare offers a unique service: it allows the child to be cared for in a setting similar to the one they are used to at home and encourages the continuity of care which is so important for a child's well-being.

The aim of this book is to provide a detailed and comprehensive guide for all aspects of working with children in a home-based setting. It will be particularly useful to both childminders and nannies.

It has been written both for people who are thinking of providing a home-based childcare service and for those who are experienced as childminders and nannies and are looking to refresh their knowledge or further their professional development.

For those who are thinking of becoming a childminder, Chapter 1 guides you through all you should know and consider in choosing this as a career. Chapter 2 offers practical information on the qualifications required to become a childminder and the support networks you can join to guide you through both your training and the early years of your career. This chapter also provides information for those who are qualified and looking to continue their professional development through further training, by registering with the appropriate networks in order to keep on top of changes in the profession, or by becoming a trainer yourself for others who are embarking on a career in home-based childcare. Chapter 3 provides full information on what a new childminder must do to both register with Ofsted and meet their requirements during inspections. Chapters 4 to 12 are a guide to becoming a true professional. They give advice on everything from choosing suitable toys and negotiating contracts with parents, to health and safety, equal opportunities and child protection. Both new and qualified readers should find this information useful to dip into. In Chapters 13 to 15 advice is given on the daily routine, including your role in children's care, learning and play; combining the care of children of different ages and needs; and behaviour management.

For those working towards the Diploma in Home-Based Childcare (DHC) to become a childminder this book provides full coverage of all you need to know to achieve this qualification: there are boxes throughout to show which DHC Units and National Standards each chapter covers. For those who are taking the same or similar qualification(s) to become a nanny (someone working in the home of the child(ren) in their care, rather than in their own home), there are boxes for information unique to this role. For those in Scotland, Wales and Northern Ireland, you should find almost all of the content relevant and there are pointers as to where you might find further information specific to your training requirements. For those in other countries, the majority of content should, again, be relevant – just ignore the boxed information regarding the DHC, and perhaps only skim through Chapters 2 and 3.

Exercises and case studies are included to develop the carer's professional skills, and extra advice is given on these at the back of the book.

Childminders and nannies offer a very valuable service to an enormous number of children and their parents. The job, whilst responsible and demanding, is also extremely rewarding; there is nothing more challenging and stimulating than providing care and education for our next generation. In writing this book I have drawn on my own years of experience as a childminder and support childminder and I hope I have managed to give practical and useful advice throughout that will be of help and inspiration to others.

As in any profession, it is essential to remember that we can never have enough knowledge and we should always be looking for ways to increase both our skills and professionalism. The more skills and qualifications we gain, the better the service we can offer. You, like the children you are caring for, never stop learning!

Acknowledgements

I would like to thank the following people for their assistance in the writing of this book:

HMSO's Licensing Division for their kind permission to reproduce core material from Ofsted publications.

June Davidson, tutor at Huddersfield Technical College, for her advice on material required for training courses.

Childminding Support Officer Rachael Flesher, and her colleagues in Harrogate, North Yorkshire, for their ideas and suggestions.

The parents and carers of the children who agreed to allow me to use photographs of their children in this book.

Choosing Childminding as a Career

National Standards
- Standard 1 – Suitable Person

Units of the Diploma in Home-based Childcare
- Unit 1 – Introduction to Childcare Practice (Home-based) (How to market your childcare service effectively)
- Unit 3 – The Childcare Practitioner in the Home-based Setting (Marketing and managing your childcare service)
- Unit 4 – Working in Partnership with Parents in the Home-based Setting (Factors influencing parents choice of childcare)

What makes a good childminder?

What exactly is a childminder? Not so very long ago childminders were viewed as just that – someone who minds children. Even today many people, when asked what a childminder does, would inevitably describe them as a person who looks after someone else's children in their own home; someone who keeps an eye on the children while their parents are at work. Although this definition is not actually false, neither is it an accurate description of the work that registered childminders carry out.

In today's society, where many parents return to work after having had children, the demand for good quality childcare is very high. Some parents prefer a home-based setting over a nursery environment for their children, and this is where childminders come into their own.

A childminder is a person who can provide a warm, loving environment; someone who is capable of providing consistent childcare, from birth and continuing throughout the child's school years, and forming a stable, trusting relationship with both the child and parent.

Registered childminders are highly skilled professionals who provide opportunities for the children in their care to learn and develop, and they should actively encourage each child to reach their full potential. They provide a very valuable service to an enormous number of children and their parents.

One of the main reasons a person chooses to become a childminder is probably because of their love of children. However, although this is obviously a very important prerequisite for the job, there are also many other aspects to consider before embarking on a career as a childminder. Despite the many benefits and advantages of becoming a childminder, it is also important to look at the disadvantages and pitfalls you may encounter.

Advantages of childminding

- You are your own boss
- You have the flexibility of working from your own home
- You can indulge your passion for working with children
- You can set your own routine
- You can decide on days and hours you wish to work
- You can set your own rates of pay
- Job satisfaction is high and working with children is very rewarding
- The work is varied and interesting.

Disadvantages of childminding

- It can have a negative effect on your own family life
- It can be a lonely profession
- It can be stressful
- You may be working long hours for low pay
- Children can be demanding, messy and noisy!
- It requires a high level of commitment
- Some training is essential
- Earnings are limited until you have built your business up.

Exercise

List as many advantages and disadvantages you can think of with regard to working as a childminder from your own home. From your own list do the pros outweigh the cons?

There are many aspects to the role of childminder and, like all professionals, it takes a certain kind of person to fulfil the role adequately. In addition to the very obvious criteria of needing to be good with children and to enjoy their company you need to have certain other attributes in order to become a successful childminder, namely:

- Be kind and considerate
- Be flexible
- Be open and approachable
- Be honest and reliable
- Be organized
- Be in good health.

The parents of the children you care for will be putting a lot of trust in you. They will probably have made one of the most important decisions of their life when choosing childcare and it is your duty to prove to them that by placing their child in your care they have made the right decision. You must not let them down. Parents may come to view you as one of the family. Not only will you be a trusted carer for their child, but also you may become a life-long friend and confidante. Parents may seek your advice and it is very important that you cherish and build on the relationship you have with both the child and their parent(s) as it is this partnership that ultimately makes your business a success. It is important that you remember that caring for children is a partnership. You must work together with the child's parents or carers to ensure that you *both* provide for the child's needs.

Figure 1.1

> ### Exercise
> Make a list of the attributes which you consider will be of benefit to you when working as a childminder.

> ### Further Information
> Unit 4 of the Diploma in Home-based Childcare – Working in Partnership with Parents in the Home-based Setting – will look at factors which influence parents' decisions when choosing childcare.

What are the implications for my own home and family life?

Childminding in your own home will inevitably have an impact on all the people living with you. For example, your partner may be out at work for most of the day or your children may be at school but there will be times in the day when they will be around while you are carrying out your childminding duties and these times can be stressful. You must remember that not all members of your family may be as tolerant of children as you are and may find the noise and mess that they make difficult to accept. It is important that you discuss with *every* member of your family the implications that running a childminding business from home may have on their life, and that of the family as a whole. It is certainly not impossible to ensure that your business runs smoothly, hand in hand with your own family commitments, but you must think carefully about the way that childminding might influence your home and family life, and work out suitable solutions which are acceptable to everyone. For example, how would you ensure that your fifteen-year-old has an adequate and quiet space to study for their forthcoming GCSEs? How would your partner feel if they found the two-year-old you are childminding scribbling all over the speech they had carefully prepared for a meeting that morning? These are situations which need to be addressed and, with careful planning, solutions for most everyday scenarios can be worked out, *providing* you have the cooperation of your entire family.

Case Study 1

Childminder Angela has a sixteen-year-old son, Andrew, who is studying for his GCSEs. Andrew is concerned that he will find studying difficult when his mum is working as the house will be noisy and the children will make it hard for him to concentrate.

Andrew discusses his concerns with his mum and together they agree to ensure that Andrew is allowed his own space to study without interruption. Andrew has agreed to keep all his study materials in his bedroom and it is agreed that none of the childminded children will be allowed to disturb him while he is studying. Angela and Andrew agree to a trial period to see how things work out. After two weeks, Andrew is happy with the arrangement and Angela notices that he comes out of his room every so often to play with the younger children as he 'winds down' after his studying.

1 Do you think Angela and Andrew found a suitable solution to the problem?
2 If they hadn't talked about the situation, what do you think may have happened?
3 What else could have been done to ensure that Angela could carry on working while her son had the chance to study?

Potential impact childminding might have on your family life

Your children will:

- have to share your affections
- have to share their toys
- be restricted as to their choice of pets
- need to be tidy and put away possessions.

However, your children will probably appreciate the added benefits that your childminding business has to offer as they will have the opportunity to:

- make lasting friendships
- mix with children from different backgrounds
- learn about a variety of cultures
- enjoy the company of both older and younger children.

Your partner may:

- be resentful of other people in your home
- be required to go through the registration checks
- have their routines disturbed if, for example, they work shifts
- find it hard having their privacy invaded
- have to refrain from smoking while you are caring for children
- be expected to help keep the house tidy and help with the chores.

Potential impact childminding may have on your home

Your home may:

- be subjected to more than the normal level of wear and tear on furniture, carpets, equipment, etc.
- incur extra costs to make both the inside and outside safe for children
- need extra cleaning

- feel cramped
- require extra storage space for prams, highchairs, play equipment, nappies, etc.

Exercise

Make a list of the implications you think a childminding business may have for each member of your family and work out a plan for dealing successfully with any problems.

Although you cannot be *too* house-proud when childminding, it is necessary for you to make everyone aware that, although you run your business from home, your childminding premises are first and foremost your *home* and as such your property must be treated with the respect it deserves. It is important to remember that everyone's ideas of acceptable and unacceptable behaviour are completely different and it is for this reason that you should implement suitable policies, which we will look at in further detail later in this book.

Children, and indeed their parents, must be informed of what you will and will not tolerate in your home and you must stick to your rules to avoid confusion and inconsistency. If, for example, you do not allow your own children to wear their outdoor footwear indoors, then it is perfectly reasonable to expect any childminded children to abide by these same rules. Likewise it is important that the children, and their parents, are aware of your rules, for example, no jumping on furniture, tidying up toys after use, etc.

It is inevitable that your home will be subjected to a lot more wear and tear while you are running your childminding business. There will be the occasional accident where things will get broken or spilt and, of course, if you are caring for babies, they may frequently vomit. Potty training children may have occasional accidents. These are all situations which you will have to contend with. There are various tax benefits and claimable expenses which can be offset against the inconvenience of the wear and tear that childminding brings to your home and we will look at these later in the book.

Exercise

You will probably already have a set of 'house rules' which your own family lives by. They may be simple things like removing shoes when coming indoors. Make a list of the things you would object to, and which may impact on your home environment.

Is there a need for the service in my area?

So, you have decided you want to be a childminder. You have looked into the implications childminding will have for your own family and home life, and you have decided that you have the right attributes to make a successful childminder. The next step is of course to look at whether your service will be a viable one. There is absolutely no point in spending a fortune on toys and equipment, registering with your regulatory body, enrolling on courses, etc. if there is no call for a childminding service in your area.

The area where you live will have a massive impact on how successful your business becomes. If you live in a rural area with very few families around you, you will have a problem filling your vacancies. Living in an area where few mothers return to work will be equally unsuccessful. It is therefore important to do your homework and research the type of childcare already available in your area, how much demand there is for childcare, and whether or not you can build a business which can successfully compete with existing childcare services and fulfil the necessary requirements.

Points to consider:

- How many other childminders are already practising in your area?
- Are the other childminders full or are they having difficulty filling their places?
- How many enquiries have they received in the past six months?
- Are there many private nurseries in your area?
- Are there any really good sought-after schools in your area?
- Do you live on a bus route?
- Are there any plans for a new housing development close to you?

All these points will have an impact on your business and you must take into consideration the answers to these questions if your business is to be successful.

How many other childminders are already practising in your area?
Contact your local authority for information about childminders in your area and ask your local childcare coordinator about the number of enquiries they have received recently.

Are the other childminders full or are they having difficulty filling their places?
You will be able to find out about the vacancies other childminders have and if they are experiencing any difficulty filling their places by asking around.

How many enquiries have they received in the past six months?
Also ask around to find out how many enquiries other childminders have had recently.

Are there many private nurseries in your area?

If there are several private nurseries in your area don't let this put you off. The fact that there are several nurseries points to a high demand for childcare. You will, of course, need to bear in mind the services that these nurseries offer but rest assured that parents looking for a childminder will have already considered the possibility of a private nursery. There are many reasons why parents opt for a childminder over a nursery. The two differ considerably and although you will have to ensure that your prices are competitive, it is highly unlikely that having private nurseries in your vicinity will have an adverse effect on your own childminding business.

Are there any really good sought after schools in your area?

Living in an area which has one or more sought-after school can prove advantageous for childminders. Taking to and collecting from schools is a service very few private nurseries offer and therefore childminders have the advantage. If you live near to a good school it is vital that you consider caring for school-aged children. Even if you prefer to care only for babies or toddlers to begin with it is highly likely that the parents who come to you for childcare will require you to continue to care for their child when they have started school. It is pointless having the advantage of living in the catchment area of a good school if you are not willing to provide before- and after-school care.

Do you live on a bus route?

If your home is near to a good bus route this could also be beneficial to your business. Not all parents drive, nor do they have the luxury of two cars, and being able to access your service by bus could be a deciding factor for them.

Are there any plans for a new housing development close to you?

New houses are being built all the time. If you hear of a new development in your area that is providing family homes this is an added bonus as there will be a whole new market for you to target.

When you have done your homework and looked into the existing childcare already available in your area you will be better equipped to decide what kind of service you are going to offer. You will need to take into consideration all the other available services and make sure that your own childminding service is both unique and competitive.

It is worth bearing in mind that the Childcare Act 2006 places a duty on all local authorities to provide sufficient childcare to meet the needs of all families. The Act also requires the development of the Early Years Foundation Stage, a framework to support the delivery of integrated care and education for babies and children under the age of 5 years.

The benefits of childminding

Earlier in this chapter we looked at what makes a good childminder and the implications that childminding can have for your home and family life. Hopefully after reading this chapter and carrying out the exercises, you will have reaffirmed in your own mind why you have decided to become a childminder.

While it is not essential to be a parent yourself in order to become a good childminder it is sensible to have some knowledge of how children develop and behave at different ages. Obviously, by being a parent yourself you will have invaluable hands-on experience of caring for a baby and young child but this is by no means the only way you can gain experience. You need to ask yourself whether you have the right qualities for such a nurturing, and often demanding, role and whether you are the type of person who can tolerate children who are noisy and messy. You need to be firm but patient, and most importantly you need to understand and be responsive to the many different ways that parents bring up their children. You must listen to the views of others and retain an open mind at all times.

The benefits of childminding are wide and varied. If you have chosen your career carefully and planned your business from the outset, the benefits should be immense. The sheer satisfaction of caring for and helping young children is in itself one of the best rewards the job has to offer. Children are often funny and creative, and childminding offers you the chance to enjoy their qualitites and assist with a child's development and learning. As a childminder your work will be varied, rewarding and fulfilling and you most certainly will never be bored!

By making good friends with the parents and becoming a valued part of their family you will enjoy another benefit of being a childminder. When caring for a child over a number of years you will become a trusted friend and be able to take satisfaction from the knowledge that you have worked in partnership with the child's parents to provide the best possible start in life for them. You will get to know a child's strengths and weaknesses, anticipate their needs, and understand their fears and anxieties. In return you will become a friend who is dearly loved and who provides a secure, happy environment for them while their parents are at work.

Exercise

Think about your own objectives for wanting to become a childminder. What are your goals and how would you like to see your business develop over the next year? What benefits do you consider childminding has to offer to your lifestyle?

Other types of childcare in a home-based setting

Before deciding whether childminding is actually the route you wish to take, it may be beneficial for you to look at the other types of childcare on offer in the home setting. You may have decided that a career working with young children is definitely something that appeals to you, however the implications of working in your own home could dissuade you from taking this option. If this is the case perhaps you might like to consider other forms of childcare where you work in the child's home.

Live-in nanny

A live-in nanny lives with the family they are working for and is usually provided with food and accommodation. Live-in nannies should work five days a week and receive two full days off. They may be expected to provide a babysitting service in the evenings, in addition to their usual working hours, and this should be negotiated with the parents. A live-in nanny should not work more than 12 hours a day (excluding babysitting).

Live-out nanny

A daily nanny, who does not live in the same house as the family they are working for, comes to the family home each day to care for the children during the set working hours agreed with the parent(s). Salaries for a daily nanny are usually a lot higher than those for a live-in nanny as food and accommodation is not provided. Live-out or daily nannies should not work for more than ten hours a day.

Temporary nanny

You may like to consider offering your services as a temporary nanny. Temporary nannies must be flexible and prepared to work on both a live-in or live-out basis. Temporary nannies can often command higher rates of pay as they are available at short notice, perhaps to cover emergencies or when the family's usual nanny is unavailable due to illness or holidays.

Special needs nanny

Often, a nanny who provides care for a child with special needs will require additional training in order to meet the needs of the child they are employed to care for. The job of a special needs nanny may be stressful and involve greater responsibility if they are dealing with specific conditions or disorders.

Au pair

Au pairs are young, single people who work abroad to study and learn about another culture and way of life. They live with the family who employs them and usually look after children, in addition to carrying out light domestic duties. Au pairs do not have contracts like other childcare practitioners. They should not be expected to work for more than five days per week and must be allowed to attend, for example, language classes. Au pairs are very different from nannies and often have little or no training in childcare. For this reason, they should not be left in sole charge of children under the age of three years. In return for the work that they do, au pairs should be provided with live-in accommodation, full board and a weekly allowance.

Mother's help

Like au pairs, a mother's help will probably not have any formal childcare qualifications and they are usually employed to work alongside mothers. A mother's help may be employed on either a live-in or live-out basis and they are particularly helpful for mothers who work from home. In addition to helping to care for the children, a mother's help will also carry out light household duties.

Maternity nurse

Maternity nurses are usually employed to help the mother of a new baby for anywhere between 4 and 12 weeks after the birth. They are usually trained and experienced nurses or nannies with special experience in caring for newborn babies. Maternity nurses are self-employed and usually live with the family in order to care for the baby through the night. Maternity nurses can be particularly helpful for mothers who have had multiple births or difficult deliveries.

Summary

At the end of this chapter you should be able to:

- Determine whether a career in childminding is for you.
- Understand the implications that childminding can have for your home and family life.
- Know how to research the childminding market in your area.
- Be aware of the competition you are up against.
- Be sure of the differences between types of home-based childcare and be able to decide which career path is right for you.

Further Reading

You can get more information about childminding by requesting a copy of 'Childminding is it for you?' from Ofsted (Tel.: 0845 601 4771)

Useful Websites

www.childminding.org
The Scottish Childminding Association (SCMA)

www.csiw.wales.gov.uk
Care Standards Inspectorate for Wales (CSIW)

www.ncma.org.uk
The National Childminding Association (NCMA)

www.nicma.org
The Northern Ireland Childminding Association (NICMA)

www.ofsted.gov.uk/about/childcare
Ofsted website

You can get more information about nannies by contacting:

www.nanniesatwork.co.uk
Nannies at Work Limited

www.nannyjob.co.uk

Becoming a Childminder and Continuing Professional Development

2

National Standards
- Standard 1 – Suitable Person

And the following units of the Diploma in Home-based Childcare
- Unit 1 – Introduction to Childcare Practice (Home-based)
- Unit 3 – The Childcare Practitioner in the Home-based Setting (Continuing professional development)

Having looked at the other options available for working with children, you should now be clear in your mind that childminding is for you. Firstly, to dispel the myths, childminding is not an 'easy option' where you can earn a wage for doing next to nothing while the children are sat in front of the television! Childminding is an exhausting, demanding job and a huge amount of commitment and responsibility comes with it. You need to be sure in your own mind that it is the career for you before you start to take on children, in order to ensure that they receive the best possible start and, most importantly, continuity of care. A child can suffer greatly from having had a lot of carers in a short period of time and this may happen if childminders let a family down or prove unsuitable.

Exercise

If, after weighing up the pros and cons, you decide that childminding is not for you, perhaps you might like to consider one of the other options of caring for children in their own home, as outlined in Chapter 1, such as becoming a nanny.

If you have decided that childminding is the career for you, you will need to become registered and look at the kinds of training on offer. Chapter 3 of this book will guide you through the registration and inspection process necessary for childminding.

Qualifications

Compulsory training

Prior to January 2006, childminders were offered the Certificate in Childminding Practice (CCP), which consisted of three units, namely:

- Introducing Childminding Practice (ICP)
- Developing Childminding Practice (DCP)
- Extending Childminding Practice (ECP).

The National Childminding Association (NCMA) and the Council for Awards in Children's Care and Education (CACHE) launched an updated qualification in January 2006. This new qualification is called the Diploma in Home-based Childcare (DHC) and it is aimed at *all* home-based childcarers; it will take the place of the Certificate in Childminding Practice.

At the time of writing, childminders in England are required to complete an accredited introductory training course, within six months of their registration. In the past, most local authorities used the Introducing Childminding Practice unit of the CCP as their compulsory training, however this has been replaced by Unit 1 of the Diploma in Home-based Childcare which, although similar to the ICP, will cover a broader scope of childcare and will also cover the work of nannies and other home-based child carers, in addition to registered childminders.

In the past all childminders in Wales were required to complete the ICP, and they will now also be expected to complete the first unit of the DHC instead. In addition, childminders in Wales must have taken fire-safety training prior to registration.

At the time of writing there were no statutory requirements for childminders in Scotland and Northern Ireland to obtain any childcare qualifications prior to becoming registered, although the majority of local authority areas run pre-registration training courses. Please see contact details at the end of the chapter for the seeking of further information on training in these areas.

Further information

At present, childminders in England are required to complete an accredited introductory course in childminding practice within six months of their registration. The National Childminding Association has, however, requested that two amendments are made to *The Childcare Bill*, which is currently being reviewed by the House of Lords. These changes are:

1 Childminders must complete an accredited introductory course *before* registration.
2 Local authorities must ensure that all registered childminders are provided with approved child protection training within 12 months of their registration. The childminders themselves are obliged to undertake this training.

The finalized *Childcare Bill* is expected to gain Royal Assent in the autumn of 2006, with the new legislation coming into effect in 2008. Although the *Childcare Bill* covers both England and Wales, some sections of the bill enable the Welsh Assembly to decide on its own legislation.

All registered childminders, wherever they practice, must take a paediatric first-aid course. First-aid courses for childminders have also changed significantly over the years and it is now usually compulsory for childminders to be trained, in depth, in all areas of paediatric first-aid for a minimum of 12 hours, and this training must be updated every three years. Your local authority will be able to advise you of the specific requirements for your area and furnish you with dates and details of suitable courses.

Diploma in Home-based Childcare

The Diploma in Home-based Childcare (DHC) was launched in January 2006, and consists of five units. The units are as follows:

- Unit 1: Introduction to Childcare Practice in the Home-based setting
- Unit 2: Childcare and Child Development (0–16) in the Home-based Setting
- Unit 3: The Childcare Practitioner in the Home-based setting
- Unit 4: Working in Partnership with Parents in the Home-based Setting
- Unit 5: Planning to Meet Children's Individual Learning Needs in the Home-based Setting.

In order to achieve the full Level 3 Diploma in Home-based Childcare, all five units must be completed, however they can be taken in any order.

The first unit, Introduction to Childcare Practice, consists of 12 guided learning hours, while the remaining four units consist of 30 guided learning hours each. A certificate will be issued after each unit is completed.

Unit 1: Introduction to Childcare Practice (ICP) Home-based

This unit is for childcare practitioners who are just starting out in their chosen profession. The unit is designed to help practitioners to:

- Assess the home-based setting for risks and ensure a safe and healthy environment is provided.
- Introduce planning routines, settle children into their care and manage behaviour effectively.
- Prepare and promote good relationships with parents and other primary carers.
- Look at their responsibilities with regard to children who may be suffering abuse or neglect.
- Prepare for the setting up of their childcare service and ensure that any legal requirements are met.

Unit 2: Childcare and Child Development (0–16) in the Home-based Setting.

This unit will teach practitioners about:

- Children's development and well-being
- Promoting children's rights
- Working with disabled children and their families.

Unit 3: The Childcare Practitioner in the Home-based Setting

This unit will teach the practitioner about:

- Being reflective
- Being assertive and valuing their own self-worth
- Advertising and marketing their childcare service
- Writing and implementing policies
- Working with other professionals
- Child protection.

Unit 4: Working in Partnership with Parents in the Home-based Setting

This unit will teach the practitioner about:

- Families and different cultures
- Confidentiality
- Contracts and complaints
- Communication with parents and primary carers
- Promoting positive relationships with parents and primary carers.

Unit 5: Planning to Meet the Children's Individual Learning Needs in the Home-based Setting

This unit will teach the practitioner about:

- Meeting individual learning needs
- Preparing, implementing and evaluating plans for home-based groups of children of different ages and abilities
- Observing and assessing children's development.

In the past, students have been expected to produce an assignment after completion of the Introducing Childminding Practice. The first unit of the new Diploma is now assessed by a multiple-choice question paper. The remaining four units are assessed through assignments, and students must complete each of the units at E grade or above to gain the Diploma.

It has been recognized by the National Childminding Association (NCMA) and the Council for Awards in Children's Care and Education (CACHE) that many childminders may already be part way through their CCP or have at least completed the first unit, the ICP. In these cases NCMA advise that students who are already part way through the DCP or ECP continue studying to complete the full certificate. If however a student has completed the ICP after 1 September 2002 they will be able to APEL (accreditation of prior education and learning) the unit they have taken into the new award. This effectively means that students don't have to complete Unit 1 of the DHC, they simply have to complete the remaining four units of the new award to gain their Level 3 qualification.

Approved Home-based Childcarers

It is not possible for childminders and nannies in England to be registered by Ofsted if they only provide care for children over the age of seven years. However these people can become 'approved childcarers'.

In order to become an approved childcarer you will need to:

- Have an 'enhanced disclosure' from the Criminal Records Bureau (the same as any childminder – more information in Chapter 3)
- Hold a current first-aid certificate for babies and young children (the same as any childminder – more information in Chapter 3)
- Attend an induction course or currently hold a relevant qualification such as ICP (more information in Chapter 2)
- Pay the necessary registration fee.

Childminders who care for children over the age of seven years will need to be approved if the child's parents are claiming the childcare element of the Working Tax Credit or if they are getting any other help with the cost of their childcare fees from their employer.

Becoming approved is also a good way of promoting your business professionally and proving your commitment to the job.

Continuing Professional Development

> Units 1 and 3 of the Diploma in Home-based Childcare relate to the need for practitioners to continue their professional development, training and quality assurance.

National Vocational Qualifications (NVQs) for childminders

It is important, as a childminder, to recognize the need to regularly update and expand on your qualifications and there are a number of courses available which can greatly enhance your training.

The National Vocational Qualification Level 3 in Children's Care, Learning and Development is a good example of a course which childminders can take to further enhance their qualifications. NVQs are nationally recognized qualifications and students working towards this award should already have gained valuable knowledge and understanding in childcare.

It is advisable for childminders to consider taking the Diploma in Home-based Childcare prior to the National Vocational Qualification Level 3 in Children's Care, Learning and Development, as the Diploma provides the underpinning knowledge required for the Level 3 NVQ.

As an NVQ is based on your actual working practice it will be necessary for your work to be assessed and for written evidence to be provided.

Nannies

At the present time there are no legal requirements for nannies to have any training qualifications. However nannies, like childminders, have a responsible role to play when caring for young children and would benefit greatly from gaining a recognized qualification. The DHC and NVQ Level 3 are both particularly suitable for nannies.

Other training courses

In addition to the recognized qualifications already mentioned, it is possible for childminders to access a variety of other training courses including workshops, conferences and seminars.

Exercise

Think carefully about the training and qualifications you already have and assess which areas of training you feel you would like to expand on. Make enquiries as to the availability of any suitable training in your area and enrol on a course which you feel would be beneficial to you in the course of your childminding work.

You may like to consider some of the following:

Child Protection Awareness Programme

This is a programme run by the National Society for the Prevention of Cruelty to Children (NSPCC) and is designed for anyone who comes into contact with children through their work or leisure activities, to raise awareness of child abuse. The programme consists of four modules, each with multiple-choice assessment. On completion of all four modules, you will be issued with a certificate. For further details and to enrol contact NSPCC (details at the end of this chapter).

Home Safety and Road Safety Programmes

The Royal Society for the Prevention of Accidents (RoSPA) runs some very informative courses designed to deal with home safety and road safety issues. RoSPA also have a variety of reasonably priced publications for sale which can be used in the course of your childminding work. For a free brochure contact RoSPA (details at the end of this chapter).

Sometimes enrolling for courses which run over a period of weeks or even months is not convenient for childminders, particularly if you are working long hours or covering parents' shift patterns. In these circumstances you may like to look into the opportunity of enrolling on a distance learning course in order to access the required training at a time to suit your own working hours. Distance learning colleges, such as ICS Ltd and the National Extension College offer a variety of courses suitable for childminders. For further information, contact details for these colleges can be found at the end of this chapter and in the useful addresses section at the back of the book.

It is important for childminders to remember the need to be 'reflective practitioners'. You should be continually striving to achieve qualifications appropriate to your business and be competent in recognizing which areas you would benefit from additional training in. Childcare is forever changing and regulations are being revised constantly. It is up to you to keep abreast of these changes and ensure that you are fully up-to-date with what is required of you as a childminder. You should never consider your training as being complete. No one can know too much, and for your business to continue to thrive and move forward you must be constantly looking for ways to improve your service.

It is not strictly necessary for childminders to continue with their training, provided they have obtained their first-aid certificate (and keep this up-to-date) and attended an introductory course. If you have the necessary knowledge to meet the National Standards you will not be required to take any further training. Training should be seen as an essential part of a childminder's job, however, not least because of the benefits of adding to your skills and experience. Relevant training can prove extremely beneficial in proving your commitment to your business and may open up job opportunities.

Studying for and Achieving Qualifications

The role of childminder is demanding and varied, and the job description not only involves caring for children but also being chef, entertainer, inspector, playground supervisor, teacher, hygienist, receptionist and manager to name just a few of the responsibilities!

How you choose to study is entirely up to you and is personal to each individual. Whereas one student may prefer the social aspect of attending regular classes and may benefit greatly from group discussions, another may prefer the solitude and convenience of studying for qualifications in their own time at home. There are pros and cons for both centre-based and distance learning studying and you must look at these against your own particular circumstances before deciding which is of benefit to you.

When you have recognized which areas you require additional training in and have enrolled on a suitable course it is important to be organized and set time aside in order to study regularly. Take notes if you are studying in class and complete assignments as soon as possible after the lesson, when the information is still fresh in your mind and you have not forgotten important facts. Books can be very expensive so consider visiting the library and borrow resources as much as possible. Try making enquiries with other childminders who have already completed the course you have enrolled on, as they may be able to offer advice or loan books to you.

Birth to Three Matters Framework

The Birth to Three Matters framework is designed to support children in their earliest years. The purpose of the framework is to provide those who are responsible for the care and education of babies and children from birth to three years with the support, information and guidance they need. The framework uses the child as its focus and it identifies four 'aspects' which celebrate the skills and competences of babies and young children. There is more reference to the Birth to Three Matters Framework in Chapter 14.

Quality Assurance Schemes

The National Childminding Association runs two Quality Assurance Schemes. One for approved childminding networks – *NCMA Children Come First* – and the other aimed at individual childminders – *NCMA Quality First*.

NCMA Children Come First

This is a quality assurance scheme designed for childminding networks who are formal groups of childminders who are managed by a paid network coordinator. Following the Government's commitment to making childminding networks an integral part of childcare, the National Childminding Association re-launched the *Children Come First* scheme in October 2005, following an extensive review. There are currently over 250 childcare networks across the country, which hold *Children Come First* approval and this number is set to rise. We will look at childminding networks in more detail later in this chapter.

Quality First

This is a quality assurance scheme designed for individual childminders in England, Wales, Scotland and Northern Ireland and it helps childminders to demonstrate that their childminding service has been checked and is of a high quality. The award is nationally recognized and shows the high standard of individual childminding practices. Although there are no minimum qualifications necessary to enrol on the scheme, participants should have some experience of childminding. The *Quality First* award can be achieved at three different levels depending on the knowledge and experience of each individual childminder. Some practitioners may find it useful to complete some or all of the units of the Diploma in Home-based Childcare prior to enrolling on the *Quality First* scheme. To achieve Quality

Figure 2.1

Assurance at level 3 you will probably have completed the full DHC or NVQ3 in Children's Care, Learning and Development prior to attempting this level. A childminder embarking on NCMA's *Quality First* will receive a set of materials which they work through, at their own pace, at home, to create a portfolio. The portfolio should take several months to complete (not usually more than a year) and it is then sent off to be assessed. An appointment is also made for a different assessor to visit the childminder and observe them during their normal working practice. The award is valid for three years after which the childminder can apply for renewal.

Support Childminding

Support Childminders are working childminders who have volunteered to help individuals who are either:

- Thinking about becoming a childminder
- Working their way through their registration or
- Are newly registered.

Support Childminders are available to newly registered childminders for up to a year into their chosen career and they can offer lots of help and advice by drawing on their own experience. Local authorities have received funding from the government to develop support childminding schemes and many new childminders or individuals going through the registration process have found the help and advice they have received from their Support Childminder invaluable. If you are interested in becoming a Support Childminder contact your local authority and enquire about vacancies in your area.

Childminding Networks

There are many informal childminding networks which are often organized through local childminding groups. These networks can be invaluable in providing support and friendship in what can, at times, be a rather lonely profession. The National Childminding Association together with the Department for Education and Employment (DfEE) expanded on these informal networks by developing the *Children Come First Quality Assurance Network Scheme*. If a network operates to a specific set of quality standards it may gain approval under the NCMA scheme. The benefits of becoming approved under this scheme are great. A coordinator is employed to work with the childminders to assess and monitor them, and to ensure that the childminders receive relevant training to expand their skills and offer a high quality standard of childcare.

Childminding networks may vary considerably. They could specialize in one particular type of service or they could combine a variety of services such as:

- Providing community childminding places for children with special needs
- Providing before- and after-school and school holiday cover
- Providing childcare for young parents
- Providing childcare for families of children who may be classed as 'in need'.

Nannies

Networks are essential for people working alone in what can, at times, be a very lonely profession. Childminders usually have the support of their local authority networks and it is also advisable for nannies to seek support, perhaps by contacting a local group. The Internet may be helpful in tracking down suitable networks. If there are none in your area, consider setting one up yourself. Support groups are invaluable for:

- Making new friends
- Sharing ideas about childcare
- Discussing your opinions about your role as a nanny.

Accredited Childminders

A childminder who is part of a NCMA *Children Come First Approved Childminding Network* and who can prove that they can meet the additional criteria in the NCMA Quality Charter may become accredited. The Quality Charter involves the promotion of the Early Learning Goals for the Foundation Stage. Once a childminder has become accredited they will be eligible for education grants payable to providers of early education for three and four-year-olds.

The National Childminding Association

The National Childminding Association (NCMA) is the only national charity and membership organization that speaks on behalf of registered childminders in England and Wales. The NCMA works in partnership with the government and the Welsh Assembly, local authorities, Early Years Development and Childcare Partnerships, Ofsted and other childcare organizations, and aims to ensure that all registered childminders have the necessary support they need to carry out their work to a high standard and that they have access to training and information.

The NCMA was founded in 1977 by a small group of registered childminders. By 2004 the association had almost 50,000 members and some 400 members of staff.

Prior to 1974 the responsibility for registering childminders was left to local authority health departments and health visitors. In 1974 this was transferred to the new social services departments who employed specialist staff to conduct childminding registration.

At around the same time a well-known educationalist, Brian Jackson, conducted a research study into the incidence of illegal childminding in two cities, Huddersfield and Manchester. The ensuing publicity surrounding Jackson's study pointed out that a large number of children were being cared for in very poor circumstances, by poorly educated, low-paid childminders who were receiving a sub-standard level of support from local authorities.

The study 'Is childminding good or bad for children?' produced a fierce debate and the public image of childminding was affected by the stigma of low childcare standards. Despite the findings, Jackson himself supported childminders and recognized that they provided a community run service for working-class children and that the majority of childminders provided high standards of care, despite poor pay and support. Jackson recommended that childminders receive better pay and conditions and wider recognition for the important role they play in society through the introduction of a Childminder's Charter.

Jackson went on to initiate three National Childminding Conferences in which childminders from all over the country had the opportunity to meet for the first time. By 1977 a number of registered childminders had formed groups to try to improve the image of childminding and campaign for better pay and conditions. At around the same time the BBC invited childminders to have their say on what they would like from a national association on a programme called *Other People's Children*. Shortly after, the National Childminding Association's membership magazine *Who Minds?* was first published.

Originally, the NCMA covered the UK but the differing legal systems in Scotland and Northern Ireland made it preferable for sister organizations to be set up. The Scottish Childminding Association (SCMA) and the Northern Ireland Childminding Association (NICMA) undertake the support in these areas.

Today the NCMA works hard to promote childminding in a variety of ways, and the poor opinion of childminding is largely a thing of the past. There are many benefits of becoming a member of the NCMA and I myself have been a member since I first registered as a childminder many years ago. In addition to special offers and discounted rates on certain products, negotiated by the NCMA, you will also receive a copy of the magazine *Who Minds?* every three months. The magazine is a useful source of information and contains up-to-date details on government policies, health and safety news, childminding news and special offers.

All members of the NCMA are entitled to purchase products and equipment that are useful for the smooth running of a childminding business at discounted rates. Products such as Inland Revenue approved cash books, medical records, receipt books, accident books, training aids and advertising packages can all be purchased through the NCMA. There is also a free information helpline available for members, offering help and advice on all aspects of childminding, including pay and conditions, contracts, child abuse allegations, etc.

How to become a childminder: summary

- Apply to the appropriate governing body for your area:
  - Office for Standards in Education (Ofsted) in England
  - Care Standards Inspectorate for Wales (CSIW)
  - Care Commission for Scotland or
  - Health and Social Services Trust for Northern Ireland
- Obtain an information pack from the appropriate authority and complete and return the forms.
- Undergo checks to ascertain your suitability as the applicant and any assistants you intend to employ.
- Checks will also be carried out on members of your household who are over the age of 16 (England, Wales and Scotland) and over the age of 10 if you live in Northern Ireland to establish their suitability to be around young children.
- An inspection of your home will be carried out to establish if it is safe and suitable for you to offer a childminding service from.
- A decision is made with regard to your registration. The length of time taken from the initial application stage through to final registration varies depending on each area and the number of checks being made, however a decision is usually reached between 3–6 months after an application has been made. Although this may seem like a long time, you will be expected to use this time to seek out appropriate first-aid training and childcare courses, in addition to getting your premises ready and familiarizing yourself with the appropriate standards for your area.

Summary

At the end of this chapter you should:

- Be aware of the compulsory training required for childminders in your area.
- Have knowledge of the training available to further enhance your qualifications.
- Know where to go for further information on training for childminders.
- Be capable of organizing your time in order to study and complete assignments.
- Understand the role of childminding networks.
- Explain the role of the National Childminding Association and identify what it has to offer.
- Be aware of the necessary steps to follow to become a registered childminder.

Further Reading

Jackson's research study was taken from information supplied by The National Childminding Association (NCMA)

Who Minds? magazine is published by the National Childminding Association

Useful Websites

www.cache.org.uk
Council for Awards in Children's Care and Education (CACHE)

www.carecommission.com
Scottish Commission for the Regulation of Care

www.childminding.org
The Scottish Childminding Association

www.csiw.wales.gov.uk
Care Standards Inspectorate for Wales (CSIW)

www.icslearn.co.uk
ICS is a distance learning college

www.ncma.org.uk
National Childminding Association (NCMA)

www.nec.ac.uk/courses
National Extension College (NEC)

www.nicma.org
The Northern Ireland Childminding Association (NICMA)

www.nspcc.org.uk
National Society for the Prevention of Cruelty to Children (NSPCC)

www.rospa.com
Royal Society for the Prevention of Accidents (RoSPA)

Registration and Inspection

3

The information in this chapter directly relates to:
- Standards 1–12 of the National Standards
- Units 1–5 of the Diploma in Home-based Childcare

The role of Ofsted

The role of Ofsted is to regulate childminding, and there are four ways in which they do this:

- Registration
- Inspection
- Investigation
- Enforcement.

Registration

This process involves checks being carried out on you, the childminder, your premises and any other people over the age of 16, (ten if you live in Northern Ireland) who will work with you to look after children, or who live with you on the childminding premises.

By registering all childminders the regulatory body aims to:

- Protect children
- Ensure that childminders meet the National Standards
- Promote a high quality provision of care and learning
- Provide reassurance for parents
- Ensure that children are safe and well cared for
- Ensure that children take part in activities that help to contribute to their learning and development.

Inspection

Once you have become registered your childminding business will be inspected by a childcare inspector periodically to ensure that your premises and working practice conform to the standards set out by the regulating body. A written report of your inspection will be sent to you and you should make this available to parents.

Investigation

Childcare inspectors have the power to carry out an investigation in order for them to check that you meet the National Standards and other requirements set out on your registration certificate.

Enforcement

If the childcare inspector finds that you do not meet the National Standards and other requirements they have the power to take action against you.

Summary

The role of Ofsted can, at times, seem a little confusing. Often childminders are unsure whether they should contact Ofsted or their local authority with regard to certain issues.

In general Ofsted's role for childminding includes the following criteria:

- Offer help and advice with completing application forms
- Work closely with the local authority in order to ensure that registration proceeds smoothly
- Deal with complaints, investigations and enforcement. Ofsted do not always visit the childminder following a complaint; this depends on the nature of the individual situation.
- Carry out inspections
- Issue inspection reports on the service childminders provide
- Retain records of the numbers of children each childminder cares for.

Ofsted DO NOT offer advice and support to childminders with regard to registration and inspection visits.

It is necessary for childminders to contact Ofsted in the following circumstances:

- If you wish to request a change in the number of children you are registered to care for.
- If you have experienced any incidents with the parents of the children you are caring for, e.g. a complaint.
- If you have had to take a child to hospital or if a child has suffered a serious injury while in your care.
- If you have suffered any serious illness or an accident.
- If you have harmed a child.
- If any child in your care has died.
- If you have any concerns regarding child protection issues.
- If you have any allegations of abuse made against yourself or any members of your family.
- If you or anyone in your family has been convicted of a criminal offence.
- If you or any members of your family have been in contact with any notifiable diseases.
- If there have been any changes to the adults living or working on your premises or if any of your own children have reached 16 years of age.
- If you wish to make any alterations to your childminding premises.
- If you wish to employ an assistant or work with another childminder. You should also notify Ofsted if you cease to employ an assistant or if you change assistants.
- If you yourself have another child or start caring for a new baby.
- If you introduce certain pets to the household, e.g. a dog.
- If you require any clarification with regard to the National Standards.
- If you start driving.

If you are unsure of whether or not you need to contact Ofsted then it is perfectly acceptable to contact your local authority in the first instance and they will inform you of whether or not you need to involve Ofsted. Your local authority can provide you with pre-registration information, together with support, advice and training throughout the registration process. They also keep records of all childminders, joint childminders and childminders working with assistants. Local authorities have an important role to play with regard to keeping childminders up-to-date with current legislation and practice, and they can provide information on funding. If your local authority is unable to help with a particular issue raised then they will to be able to direct you to the relevant agencies who are in a position to offer the appropriate help and support.

Nannies

At the time of writing nannies are the only childcare practitioners who are not required to undertake some form of registration. There are, however, government plans for a proposed Home Childcarers Scheme which would set out a code of practice to be monitored by Ofsted.

Who needs to register?

Anyone who looks after one or more children under the age of eight for more than a total of two hours a day, on domestic premises, for reward must be registered by Ofsted. Reward does not necessarily mean a cash payment; it could mean payment in kind.

You will not need to register with Ofsted if any of the following apply:

- You are the parent, or a relative of the child you are looking after
- You have parental responsibility for the child
- You are a local authority foster parent to the child
- You have fostered the child privately
- You only look after the child between the hours of 6pm and 2am
- You look after children for two sets of parents wholly or mainly in the home of either or both sets of parents.

Remember

If you do not fall into one of the above mentioned categories you must be registered before you can work as a childminder. It is an offence to work as a childminder without being registered, and if you do so, it could lead to prosecution.

At the time of writing the Department for Education and Skills (DfES) is consulting on a new registration process for childcarers to ensure that registration is tailored to different providers. Ofsted is proposing to administer two registers:

1 The Early Years Register – for those caring for children up to the age of five and
2 The Ofsted Childcare Register (OCR) – for those caring for children aged five years and over

If the proposals go ahead, childminders who care for children aged both under and over five years will need to register on both of the above mentioned registers. However, they will not have to go through a separate application process nor will they have to pay an additional fee to register on the Ofsted Childcare Register.

If the proposal is accepted, the Ofsted Childcare Register will begin registering nannies and over-7s childminders from April 2007 and with all those caring for children aged 5–7 years on the OCR by September 2008.

More information about this proposal can be found by visiting www.dfes.gov.uk/consultations

Requirements for registration

You will be expected to demonstrate to Ofsted the following four criteria before you can be registered :

- That you, and every other person looking after children on the premises where you intend to childmind, are suitable to look after children under the age of eight years.
- That every person living or employed on the premises where you intend to childmind is suitable to be in regular contact with children under the age of eight years.
- That your premises are suitable to be used for looking after children under the age of eight years.
- That you comply with the National Standards, regulations and any conditions which Ofsted may feel the need to impose.

In addition to the National Standards and any conditions that may be imposed on you during your registration, you will also have to meet other requirements, including informing Ofsted of:

- Any changes to your premises and childcare provision
- Any changes to the people living or working on your premises and their suitabillity
- Any matters affecting the welfare of children in your care.

There are certain things that would automatically prevent you from becoming a childminder and these are:

- If you have been convicted or charged with any offence against a child.
- If you have been convicted or charged with certain offences against an adult.
- If you are listed on the Protection of Children Act List. This list consists of people considered unsuitable to work with children.
- If you are listed in information held under Section 142 of the *Education Act 2002* (formerly known as List 99).

Applying for registration

The flow chart in Figure 3.1 details the steps of the Ofsted application process.

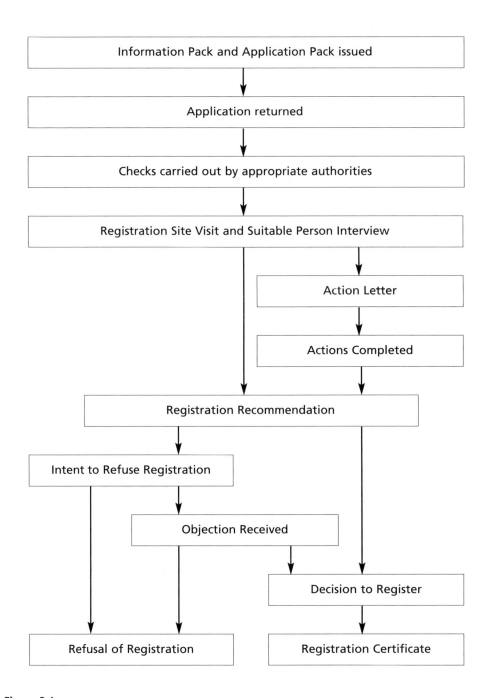

Figure 3.1

Case Study 2

Anne is going through the process of becoming a registered childminder. She has returned the relevant forms and has an appointment scheduled for an inspector to carry out her suitable person interview. Through word of mouth, Anne receives a telephone call enquiring about a childcare place, to start immediately. The person making the enquiry tells Anne that they are confident that she will be granted registration and that they are willing to sign a contract for her to begin to care for their child before registration has been granted. Anne explains to the parent that this will not be possible as she would be breaking the law if she began childminding before gaining the necessary permission. Anne explained that she had an appointment to see an inspector and agreed to telephone the parent after she had spoken to the inspector to give them some idea of how long it would be before she would be allowed to start childminding.

1 Do you think Anne did the right thing?
2 What problems might Anne have been faced with if she had agreed to take the child prior to registration?

Ofsted will usually inform you within three months of receiving an application whether or not you will be allowed to become registered. Many of the processes, however, require information from other agencies as well as actions that you may be required to take, and therefore completion of some of the stages may result in a delay in processing your application. If this is the case Ofsted will inform you. Let us now look at the flow chart in greater detail.

Information and Application Pack Issued

You must contact your local authority to obtain an information pack. At this point your local authority will give you details of a pre-registration briefing session and further information about registration courses and training. If you have not already received a copy of the National Standards and Guidance to the Standards then you should also request these when applying for your information pack. It is important that you familiarize yourself with the National Standards before you apply to become registered. The application pack will contain general information with regard to childminding and the registration process. The pack will also contain the relevant forms for you to complete and return.

Remember

Complete all the necessary forms and return them with the appropriate *original* documents requested.

Registration Site Visit and Suitable Person Interview

It is completely understandable for you to feel apprehensive about your forthcoming visit from an Ofsted inspector. It is important, however, to remember that the inspector is not working *against* you and that they are looking for reasons to *register* you. The inspector's aim is to determine whether or not you have the necessary aptitude to work with young children. They will inform you of any improvements they feel you will need to make prior to registration and they will offer help and advice when necessary.

> **Exercise**
>
> Before your inspection visit make sure you are familiar with the National Standards, and think about the ways you will meet these Standards while carrying out your childminding duties.

Action Letter

If the inspector feels that changes need to be made to your premises, following the site visit, then you will receive an action letter. The purpose of the action letter is to inform you of any changes which the inspector feels need to be made prior to granting registration.

Decision To Register

Ofsted will notify you in writing of their decision to register you as a childminder. You will be required to pay the registration fee and provide written acceptance of any conditions imposed on your recommendation for registration.

Registration Certificate

Your registration certificate will contain your name and address, the number of children you are registered to care for and any conditions imposed with regard to your registration. This certificate is your proof of registration, and it is a mandatory requirement that you display the certificate at all times when you are carrying out your childminding duties. If you decide that you no longer wish to work as a registered childminder, you must return the certificate to Ofsted.

Intent to Refuse Registration, Objection and Refusal

In some circumstances Ofsted may issue a notice of intention to refuse your application. This would only happen if it is felt that you do not meet all the requirements for registration. The notice of intention to refuse your application will include any reasons Ofsted feel necessary to impose a refusal. If you wish to object against Ofsted's decision with regard to their refusal of your application then you must do this in writing within 14 days of receipt of your 'intent to refuse registration' letter. If you do not make any objection then Ofsted will assume that you do not wish to continue with the registration process and they will then issue a letter confirming their refusal in writing. Any further right to appeal would have to go to an independent tribunal.

Inspections

From April 2005 Ofsted changed the way it carries out inspections of childcare and nursery education. With regard to childminders, Ofsted will inspect and report on the 'quality and standards of childminding and day care'.

In order for Ofsted to make their judgement about the overall quality of the childminder's setting the inspector will ask the very important question 'What is it like for a child here?' The inspector will judge how well each childminder meets a series of outcomes for children that are set out in the *Childrens Act 2004*. These outcomes are as follows:

- How do you help children to be healthy?
- How do you protect children from harm or neglect and help them to stay safe?
- How do you help children to enjoy themselves and achieve their full potential?
- How do you help children to make a positive contribution to your setting and to the wider community?

The inspector will also judge how well you organize your childcare service in order to help promote children's well being and they will take into account whether you meet the National Standards for childminding.

Ofsted will normally inspect newly registered childminders within a short period of time after completion of their registration. After that inspections are carried out at least once every three years. However, more frequent inspections will be carried out if:

- It was felt that the last inspection showed that the quality of childcare had significant weaknesses.
- There have been significant changes since the last inspection, such as a change of premises.
- Ofsted receive information such as a complaint about a childcare service that might suggest that the National Standards are not being met.

Ofsted wish to see your setting running as normally as possible on any given day without you making any special arrangements. It is because of this that Ofsted have decided not to give specific dates for inspection visits. Childminders will be contacted by telephone a few days prior to a planned inspection to check whether there are any days in the coming week when it would not be suitable to visit. Ofsted are aware that many childminders spend a lot of their time away from the home, at support groups, doing school runs, etc. and so it has been decided that a few days notice should be given in order that an inspector does not turn up when the childminder is out.

It is important, when the inspector arrives, that you do not make any significant changes to your normal routine. Disruption must be kept to a minimum, although of course the inspector will need to speak to you during the inspection to discuss the childcare that you provide. At the beginning of the visit the inspector will discuss with you how he or she will carry out the inspection. Prior to your inspection visit, you should have received a self-evaluation form inform entitled 'What is it like for a child here?'. This self-evaluation part of the inspection was introduced in April 2005 and the Inspector will discuss with you the grades you have awarded yourself. The inspector will spend most of their time during the inspection visit observing what you and the children are doing. They will talk to the children and, if possible, the parents to find out their views on the childcare you provide. They will check the premises and equipment to ensure that these are safe and suitable and how well they are used to promote the outcomes for children. The inspector will also check records, procedures and any other documents.

The inspector will make notes throughout the inspection and, at the end of the inspection, he or she will let you know the outcome of their findings. It is usual for you to see a display of the inspectors judgements on a laptop computer and it will be these judgements that will be included in your report. At this stage you may correct any factual detail or ask for further clarification of any points the inspector may raise.

After the inspection you will receive your inspection report from Ofsted. If at this time you notice any factual inaccuracies you should notify Ofsted as soon as possible, as the report will be published soon after your inspection, on the Internet. Any points you raise will be considered and changes made when necessary. From April 2005 all early years inspection reports have been published on Ofsted's website, however in the case of childminders the report will not include your name or your full address.

Another change to the way Ofsted carries out inspections is the introduction of a new grading scale. From April 2005 changes have been made to the way childminding practices are graded with a straightforward four points grading scale now being used. The scale is used to make a judgement on how well a childminder's provision meets each of the outcomes, and is used to make an overall judgment on the quality of the childcare. The grades are as follows:

- Grade 1 – **Outstanding** – this grade is given to exceptional settings that have excellent outcomes for children.
- Grade 2 – **Good** – this grade is given to strong settings that are effective in promoting outcomes for children.
- Grade 3 – **Satisfactory** – this grade is given to settings that have acceptable outcomes for children but which have scope for improvement.
- Grade 4 – **Inadequate** – this grade is given to weak settings that have unacceptable outcomes for children.

If your childcare setting is judged by an inspector as being either **satisfactory** or **good**, the report will include recommendations to help you improve your provision further. An inspector will check whether you have acted on these recommendations at your next inspection. If you fail to meet one or more of the National Standards for childminding the inspector will judge the quality of your care as **inadequate**. If this is the case you will be sent a letter to tell you what action you must take to improve the care you provide. This letter is called a Notice of Action to Improve. When you have taken the necessary action you must inform Ofsted. Ofsted may carry out an announced or unannounced visit to check that the necessary action has been taken. If you do not take the required action or if the action you have taken has little impact Ofsted may take further enforcement measures. In any case, if you have received a Notice of Action to Improve you will receive another inspection within six to twelve months. If the childcare you provide is poor and requires immediate improvement Ofsted will take enforcement action, such as issuing a compliance notice. A compliance notice will be followed up by Ofsted to ensure that improvements have been made or, in some cases, suspension or cancellation of the registration will occur. In the cases where Ofsted takes serious action, but allows registration to continue, a further inspection will take place at the date given on any enforcement action or within three to six months, whichever is the sooner.

Although it is perfectly normal to feel a little nervous about your inspection visit, there are certain things that you can do to ensure that you are ready and that your inspection goes smoothly.

Preparing for your inspection

- Make sure you have completed the self-evaluation form.
- Make sure you have addressed any weaknesses which were identified in your last inspection report.
- Make sure that you have all the required records, namely,
    - the name, home address and date of birth of each child you look after;
    - the name, home address and telephone number of a parent of each child you care for;
    - the name, home address and telephone number of any person who will be looking after children with you;
    - a daily record of the names of the children looked after on the premises, including the hours of attendance;
    - a record of all accidents that have occurred on the premises;
    - a record of any medical products administered to any child on the premises including the date and circumstances of the administration, who administered it and a record of the parent's consent.
- Check that you and any assistants working with you are familiar with all relevant documents, including the National Standards for childminders, Ofsted's Guidance to the National Standards for Childminders, Birth to Three Matters and the Curriculum Guidance for the Foundation Stage.
- Make sure that you keep any information about how parents view your service and any improvements you have made as a result.

- Make sure you have available any record you keep of complaints about the childcare that you provide.
- Make sure that you have notified Ofsted of any significant changes to your provision, including the people looking after children or living on the premises where you carry out your childminding duties, the premises where you provide care and your own details.

If you need help in getting ready for your inspection you can receive guidance from Ofsted's website by logging on to www.ofsted.gov.uk/publications. This website gives detailed information on how Ofsted awards inspection judgements and also offers other sources of information and support. You can also contact your local authority for help and advice with regard to inspections.

The Self-Evaluation Form

Self-evaluation forms part of Ofsted's revised inspection procedure. Prior to your inspection visit you will be expected to complete a self-evaluation form. The form consists of five questions which you will be required to answer using the same grading system the inspector will use themselves.

The grading scale is as follows:

- Grade 1 – **Outstanding** – I consider my practice to be excellent
- Grade 2 – **Good** – I consider this to be a strong area
- Grade 3 – **Satisfactory** – I consider this to be OK but I could do better
- Grade 4 – **Inadequate** – I consider this to be not good enough and I know I need to improve.

The questions you will be required to answer on the self-evaluation form are as follows:

1 How effective are you in helping children to be healthy?
2 How effective are you in protecting children from harm and neglect and keeping them safe?
3 How effective are you in helping children to enjoy what they do and to achieve as well as they can?
4 How effective are you in helping children make a positive contribution to your provision and to the wider community?
5 How effective is your organization of childcare?

You will be required to answer the above questions using the four-tier grading scale mentioned above.

The National Standards and how to meet them successfully

STANDARD 1 – Suitable Person

Adults providing day care, looking after children or having unsupervised access to them are suitable to do so.

Ofsted will take into account:

- Your understanding of the National Standards and how you meet them
- Your training and experience
- Your ability to provide suitable care for the children
- Your mental and physical fitness
- The way in which you make decisions about who works with you.

STANDARD 2 – Organization

The registered person meets the required adult:child ratios, ensures that training and qualification requirements are met and organizes space and resources to meet the children's needs effectively.

Ofsted will take into account:

- That you are working within the required adult:child ratios
- How you make use of your space and resources
- How you record details of any assistants working with you
- Your attendance records for the children you look after.

STANDARD 3 – Care, Learning and Play

The registered person must meet children's individual needs and promote their welfare. They plan and provide activities and play opportunities to develop children's emotional, physical, social and intellectual capabilities.

Ofsted will take into account:

- How you choose and organize your activities
- How you relate to the children in your care
- How you encourage children to try new activities and involve them in ways which enable them to investigate and explore.

STANDARD 4 – Physical Environment

The premises are safe, secure and suitable for their purpose. They provide adequate space in an appropriate location, are welcoming to children and offer access to the necessary facilities for a range of activities which promote their development.

Ofsted will take into account:

- How you organize your resources and space
- The toilet and nappy changing facilities on offer
- The kitchen facilities on offer
- The outdoor area available.

STANDARD 5 – Equipment

Furniture, equipment and toys are provided which are appropriate for their purpose and help to create an accessible and stimulating environment. They are of suitable design and condition, well maintained and conform to safety standards.

Ofsted will take into account:

- How you ensure that your furniture, toys and equipment are safe
- How you choose toys and equipment to meet the needs of all of the children
- How you promote equality of opportunity through the use of toys and play materials
- The accessibility of toys and equipment to all the children.

STANDARD 6 – Safety

The registered person takes positive steps to promote safety within the setting and on outings and ensures proper precautions are taken to prevent accidents.

Ofsted will take into account:

- Your plans for fire safety and emergency evacuation
- Your smoke alarms and fire blankets
- The arrangements you make for outings
- The sleeping arrangements you have in place for the children
- How you keep your records for drivers and vehicles
- Your public liability insurance certificate.

STANDARD 7 – Health

The registered person promotes the good health of children and takes positive steps to prevent the spread of infection and appropriate measures when they are ill.

Ofsted will take into account:

- How you keep records of accidents
- How you keep records for the administration of medication
- Consent forms for the administration of medication or emergency treatment
- Your first-aid box
- Your policy for sick children
- Your policy on smoking.

STANDARD 8 – Food and Drink

Children are provided with regular drinks and food in adequate quantities for their needs. Food and drink is properly prepared, nutritious and complies with dietary and religious requirements.

Ofsted will take into account:

- Your arrangements for providing food and drink
- How you meet children's dietary needs
- The records you keep regarding children's dietary needs.

STANDARD 9 – Equal Opportunities

The registered person and staff actively promote equality of opportunity and anti-discriminatory practice for all children.

Ofsted will take into account:

- Your understanding of equality of opportunity
- How you meet children's specific needs.

STANDARD 10 – Special Needs

The registered person is aware that some children may have special needs and is proactive in ensuring that appropriate action can be taken when such a child is identified or admitted to the provision. Steps are taken to promote the welfare and development of the child within the setting in partnership with the parents and other relevant parties.

Ofsted will take into account:

- Your arrangements for caring for children with special needs
- The records you keep with regard to the children
- How you share information about your provision for children with special needs with their parents.

STANDARD 11 – Behaviour

Adults caring for children in the provision are able to manage a wide range of children's behaviour in a way which promotes their welfare and development.

Ofsted will take into account:

- Your policy for managing behaviour
- Any records of significant incidents.

STANDARD 12 – Working In Partnership With Parents and Carers

The registered person and staff work in partnership with parents to meet the needs of the children, both individually and as a group. Information is shared.

Ofsted will take into account:

- How you inform parents about your daily routines and childcare practices
- Your written agreements with parents
- Your record of complaints
- The records you keep about the children in your care and their parents' details.

STANDARD 13 – Child Protection

The registered person complies with local child protection procedures approved by the Area Child Protection Committee (ACPC) and ensures that all adults working and looking after children in the provision are able to put the procedures into practice.

Ofsted will take into account:

- Your understanding of child abuse and neglect
- Your ability to carry out the ACPC procedures should you suspect a child in your care is being abused
- That you are capable of dealing with any allegations of abuse made against you or anyone else living or working on your childminding premises.

STANDARD 14 – Documentation

Records, policies and procedures which are required for the efficient and safe management of the provision, and to promote the welfare, care and learning of children are maintained. Records about individual children are shared with the child's parent.

Ofsted will take into account:

- What documents you keep and how you store them
- Whether you have notified them of any changes to your circumstances
- How you share information with parents and keep them informed of their child's progress.

Childminders working in Wales and Scotland will have a different set of Standards to work from.

Welsh National Minimum Standards

There are 21 minimum standards for childminders working in Wales, including working in partnership with parents, behaviour, equal opportunities, child protection and safety. More information about the Welsh National Minimum Standards can be found by contacting the Care Standards Inspectorate for Wales (details in the useful addresses section in the back of this book).

Scottish National Care Standards

Childminders in Scotland work within the boundaries of 14 standards, including promoting equal opportunities and the providing of a stimulating environment in which children are welcomed, nurtured and encouraged by supportive staff who interact effectively and enthusiastically with the children. Details of the Scottish National Care

Standards can be obtained by contacting the Scottish Care Commission (details in the useful addresses section in the back of this book).

Summary

At the end of this chapter you should:

- Understand the role of Ofsted
- Understand the aims of the registration system
- Know how to apply for registration
- Be familiar with the inspection procedure
- Understand the National Standards and how to implement them.

Further Reading

The Standards for England can be obtained from Sure Start.

The Standards for Northern Ireland can be obtained from The Northern Ireland Childminding Association (NICMA).

The Standards for Scotland can be obtained from the Scottish Commission for the Regulation of Care.

The Standards for Wales can be obtained from The Care Standards Inspectorate for Wales (CSIW).

Useful Websites

www.carecommission.com
Scottish Commission for the Regulation of Care

www.childminding.org
The Scottish Childminding Association (SCMA)

www.csiw.wales.gov.uk
Care Standards Inspectorate for Wales (CSIW)

www.ncma.org.uk
The National Childminding Association (NCMA)

www.nicma.org
The Northern Ireland Childminding Association (NICMA)

www.surestart.gov.uk
Sure Start

The Professional Childminder

4

National Standards
- Standard 12 – Working in Partnership with Parents and Carers

Units of the Diploma in Home-based Childcare
- Unit 1 – Introduction to Childcare Practice
- Unit 3 – The Childcare Practitioner in the Home-based Setting
- Unit 4 – Working in Partnership with Parents

Creating the right image for your business

Professionalism comes with experience. It is a gradual process which is developed through skills, knowledge and attitude. The professional childminder uses their skills to work in an organized way. They are non-judgemental and work objectively, and they make the most of training and other development practice in order to keep up-to-date with procedures and legislation.

In order to generate the right amount of business it is vital that you go about your work in a professional manner. First impressions are always very important and it is essential that you realize that caring for other people's children is not the same as caring for your own. Balancing self-employment from home with family life is often very difficult, and it requires a professional approach in order for it to work.

A parent has the right to expect respect and confidentiality from the childminder in much the same way as the childminder has the right to expect the same from the parent. Negotiating a contract which stipulates hours, fees, holidays and notice is a good way of showing parents your commitment to your business and ensures that both parties know exactly what is expected of them.

As a childminder it is possible that you have worked very hard to get your business up and running and you will have gone through months of training and preparation. It is essential therefore that you do yourself justice at the crucial point of getting your business up and running. There are certain things you should bear in mind when setting out to create the right image for your business:

- Always be ready for the arrival of the children in the morning
- Be polite and make both the parents and the children feel welcome
- Have a cheerful and friendly disposition
- Show patience and kindness
- Ensure that your home is clean and safe at all times
- Respect the wishes of both parents and children and listen to what they have to say
- Be discreet and honest
- Be punctual – never take children to school, nursery, etc. late
- Ensure that the records you keep are accurate and up-to-date
- Ensure that parents are kept informed of any changes to your business such as contract/fee reviews, holidays, etc. well in advance
- Make the most of any training opportunities and keep your training up-to-date
- Act responsibly at all times. Remember children learn from example and you must portray the image of a trained professional when caring for children.

As a professional you should display enthusiasm, commitment and motivation towards your business at all times. It is important that you take the time to review and evaluate your practice from time to time in order that you can assess what is or is not achievable within your setting.

Exercise

Try to identify your strengths and weaknesses. Make a list of the things you would like to change within your practice and consider attending any appropriate training.

Gaining knowledge is a vital part of being a professional childminder. With knowledge comes the ability to understand the children you care for. You will be better equipped to interpret observations and therefore spot any problems early on and you will be in a position to ensure that all children receive the help and support they need. You can never know enough. There is no end to the training a childminder can gain and you must be willing to attend courses to update your knowledge whenever necessary. There is more about training in Chapter 2 of this book.

Deciding on the kind of service to provide

There are many ways of running a successful childminding business and one childminder's service can differ greatly from the next. Before deciding on the kind of service that you wish to provide it is important to think carefully about the consequences your service may have on other aspects of your family life.

It is a good idea to discuss all aspects of your business with your own children and partner. Find out what they expect from you on a daily basis and try, as far as possible, to accommodate their wishes as they will be affected by the service you provide.

It is important from the very outset that you are clear in your mind exactly what service you are willing to provide. NEVER agree to something that you cannot deliver. Both you and the parent must be completely satisfied with the arrangement before contracts are signed or you may incur problems at a later date.

You must remember that, even after contracts have been negotiated and signed, parents may request changes to the service they require. Always be clear in your own mind what your limitations are and do not agree to any changes you are not happy with. Parents may put you on the spot at times and request your help in an emergency or as a 'one off'. It is always a good idea to accommodate changes, if possible, however never feel pressurized to agree to something if it is not a viable option from your own point of view. It is quite acceptable for you to ask for time to 'consider' a parent's proposal, and this will enable you to think carefully about any implications for your existing commitments and to talk it through with your family members if the changes are to be over a long period of time.

Exercise

In order to make sure you are able to deal with situations which may arise, it is a good idea to try to anticipate some of the problems you may encounter. Talk to other childminders and try to discover whether they have experienced any problems in their work (always remember to stay within the boundaries of confidentiality and *never* discuss a particular family's circumstances with anyone else). After making enquiries, are you aware of any patterns arising? For example, do several childminders have problems with parents collecting children late or failing to pay their fees on time? You should be able to identify the most common issues, and being aware of potential problems puts you in a good position to deal with them. You can now set about thinking how you would handle similar situations, should they happen to you.

When you have decided, with your family, the kind of daily service you feel you are able to provide which fits in around your own commitments, it is important then to give serious consideration to the actual type of childcare you are willing to offer. Some childminders prefer to care only for school-aged children while others prefer only babies and young children. The number of children you are registered to care for will, of course, have an influence over the type of day care service you can offer. Some of the things you will need to consider are:

- Are you willing to take and collect children from playgroup, nursery and school? This could have a major impact on your childminding service. Refusing to do the 'school run' may limit your market considerably.
- Are you willing to care for babies under 12 months old?
- Are you willing to care for school-aged children?
- Are you willing to work school holidays?
- Are you willing to take/collect children from clubs such as swimming, dance, drama, etc.?
- What meals are you prepared to offer? Will these meals be buffet style or cooked?
- What kind of activities and experiences are you able to provide for each age group of children?

Exercise

If you are willing to take and collect children from school, nursery and playgroup make a list of which settings you are going to concentrate on. It is important to take into account travelling time and starting times and not to overstretch yourself so that you are rushing from one school to the next in order to get children there on time.

Building a professional portfolio

Once you have become registered it is a good idea to spend some time building a portfolio about yourself and putting together a welcome pack about your business to give to potential customers.

A portfolio should consist of information about yourself and should include the following:

1 A short history about yourself, your family, your background and your experience to date.
2 A copy of your Registration Certificate.
3 A copy of your Public Liability Insurance.
4 A copy of your latest report from Ofsted or CSIW.
5 A copy of your Criminal Records Bureau (CRB) disclosure and any others for assistants and family members over the age of 16 years of age, or 10 if you live in Northern Ireland.

6   A copy of your first-aid training certificate.

7   Copies of any other relevant childcare training certificates, such as
    — Introducing Childminding Practice
    — Developing Childminding Practice
    — Extending Childminding Practice
    — Quality Assurance
    — NVQ in Children's Care Learning and Development
    — Diploma in Home-Based Childcare.
    Training certificates should be added to your portfolio as and when you have achieved
    them throughout your career.

8   Details of any seminars or workshops you have attended.

9   References from other parents who have used your service.

10 Thank you cards or letters from the children or their parents.

11 Copies of your policies.

12 Your personal emergency plan.

13 Details of the times and days your service is available.

14 Details of the fees charged.

15 Details of any holidays booked.

16 Sample menus.

17 Details of the activities and learning experiences you offer children.

18 Details of your usual daily routine; which toddler/support groups you attend.

A portfolio is a detailed record of all the information relevant to your childcare business, and it should be designed for you to go through with parents in order that you can explain its contents. A ringbinder is an ideal way of storing your portfolio as information can be added and updated easily.

In much the same way as a portfolio is designed it is a good idea to create a welcome pack for parents. A welcome pack should be much smaller than a portfolio and only contain important, relevant information. Welcome packs are intended for the parent to take away with them as a reference and guide to your service. Welcome packs should be organized and easy to read.

A welcome pack may consist of:

1   A leaflet or booklet advertising your business.

2   Details of your full name, address, telephone numbers and email address, if you have one.

3   Details of the service you provide, including the days and hours you operate.

4   Details of the schools, nurseries and playgroups you attend.

5   Details of the fees you charge and what these include.

6   Brief details of your daily routines and the activities and learning experiences you provide for the children.

7   A sample menu.

8 Details of any holidays booked.

9 A photocopy of your registration certificate.

10 A photocopy of your last inspection report (if relevant).

11 Copies of any relevant policies.

Exercise

Put together a portfolio and welcome pack to use when interviewing potential customers for your own childminding service. It is worth remembering that the information contained within the portfolio and welcome packs should be professionally displayed and create the right image!

Working in partnership with parents and carers

It is always important to remember that a child's parents or primary carers, such as grandparents, foster parents, etc. are *the* most important people in the child's life. You must remember, at all times, that parents and primary carers know their children better than anyone else and as such must be shown the respect they deserve. They are the people who will teach their children the most about their own family, its cultures and beliefs.

As a childminder it is vital that the relationship you have with the primary carers of a child you are looking after is a good one. Children can sense when there is an atmosphere and it is important that any problems that may arise are dealt with quickly and effectively. You will get to know the families of the children you are caring for very well, as they are welcomed into your home on a regular basis, and this friendship should be cherished and nurtured.

An excellent method of getting parental feedback without putting parents on the spot, is to issue questionnaires periodically. You could ask a few basic questions like:

- What aspects of my childcare service are you particularly pleased with?
- Are you satisfied with the standard of care your child receives from me?
- Are you satisfied with the meals and snacks I provide?
- Are there any aspects of my service which you feel I could improve on?

Make it clear to parents, in your questionnaire, that you value their comments and feedback and that you will endeavour to make any improvements necessary as a result of their answers. It is not always easy to please everyone, particularly if you are not even aware of parental preference, and questionnaires can be a valuable way of gaining views from individuals who may otherwise not express their opinions to you. Keep the completed questionnaires for future reference and to show to your Ofsted inspector during your inspection as they will indicate your willingness to improve the service you provide and show that you are working as a reflective practitioner.

Communication is probably the most important factor in establishing a successful relationship with parents and carers. A lack of communication can very quickly lead to misunderstanding and it is important that you are aware of the different types of communication skills.

Listening

It is important, as a childminder, to learn to become a good listener. This will require effort and concentration.

Speaking

This is probably the most effective way of communicating. It is important to think carefully before you speak and, if you have any important issues to raise with a parent or carer it is a good idea to make a few notes beforehand to remind you of all the points you wish to discuss.

Body language

This type of non-verbal communication takes place all the time when our bodies are expressing themselves. You should try to use positive body language at all times.

Writing

Some childminders are unhappy with the amount of paperwork involved in the running of their business. They may feel uncertain about their own grammar and spelling ability and are rather daunted by the prospect of maintaining records or writing reports. It is important to remember that there are many sources of help such as colleges and local groups. Investing in a computer is an excellent way of tackling any spelling and grammar problems as they often have built-in checks. A good dictionary is a must when devising policies, contracts, etc.

> ### Exercise
> Think about the ways you communicate on an everyday level. Do you consider yourself to be a good communicator? How effective are you at giving instructions or information? Make a list of any aspects you are not sure of and find out ways of improving your skills.

Very few people relish the thought of conflict, however, we are all different and we all have differing values and outlooks on life. Although, in an ideal world, it would be nice if disagreements did not occur this is neither a practical or possible situation.

> ### Further information
>
> Working in partnership with parents directly relates to Standard 12 of the National Standards and Unit 4 of the Diploma in Home-based Childcare.

Differences in opinion are vital to our own development and, because of these differences, it is important that both you and the parents of the children you care for understand the need to be flexible and make compromises. No matter how hard you try, and how well you communicate with parents and children, there may be times when the relationship you have built up breaks down. It is in the interests of everyone – you, the parent and the child – to ensure that any conflict is dealt with quickly and effectively.

Case Study 3

Childminder Anne has enrolled on a training course one evening per week. Anne's working day should finish at 6.00pm, giving her time to have her tea and get to the college for the start of the course at 6.45pm. For the past few weeks Anne has been finding it difficult to attend the course due to Ben's mum, Adele, collecting her son late from Anne's setting. Anne is having to either miss classes or turn up late and is beginning to find the situation stressful.

Anne decides to tackle the problem and, before her next class, she mentions to Adele that it will be necessary for her to collect Ben on time in order for her to get to college. Anne politely points out that she and Adele had agreed that Ben would be collected at 6.00pm and that they had both signed a contract to this effect. Anne explains her situation and adds that by collecting Ben late Adele is making it very difficult for her to attend classes. Adele agrees to make more of an effort to collect Ben on time.

1 Was Anne right to confront Adele?
2 In your opinion, did Anne tackle the situation well?
3 What could Anne do if Adele continued to collect Ben late?

While it is all too easy to think of our own needs and circumstances, it is also important that we consider the circumstances of others. To avoid the situation above it may have been easier for Anne to explain to Adele that she was enrolling on a course and that she would need Ben to be collected on time in order for her to get to the classes. If Anne has never objected to Adele's bad timekeeping in the past she should not expect Adele to anticipate problems if she has not been made aware of them. Always remember that if a parent is late it may not be their fault. No one can anticipate traffic problems or road accidents and there will be times when late collections are unavoidable. If, however, a parent is persistently late and this interferes with other arrangements you may have then it is vital that the situation is resolved amicably. Again, the delay may be unavoidable but if contracts have been agreed and are regularly breached, then either a new contract should be negotiated or collection arrangements altered. By keeping open the lines of communication and discussing any problems you should be able to avoid unnecessary conflict and reach a compromise which is suitable for everyone.

Remember

Always deal with problems in a professional manner. Explain your point of view and then listen to what others have to day. Compromises will need to be made by everyone and, by talking things through with parents, it should be possible to find a solution which is acceptable to everyone.

How to be a reflective practitioner

It is good practice for childminders to regularly reflect on their work. You should set aside time periodically to look at your own practice and think carefully about what, if any, improvements may be beneficial to your business. Ask yourself:

1 What areas of my childminding business am I particularly proud of?
2 What areas can I improve on?
3 Have I been caught out unexpectedly by anything I was unprepared for?
4 If so, did I handle the situation well or could I make improvements?
5 Have I had any recent complaints?
6 If so, what can I do to improve the areas which have given cause for complaint?

It is important that you answer these questions honestly and look at your working practice with a critical eye in order to get a true picture of things.

By asking yourself reflective questions you should be able to develop ways of building on your successes and improving any areas which have been less successful.

Working alone can make being a reflective practitioner more difficult as you only have your own ideas and opinions to work with. If you work with another childminder or employ an assistant you will be able to share ideas and seek different opinions. However, if you do work alone you could try talking to parents, other childminders, network coordinators or other childcare professionals for help in particular areas.

In order for your business to develop and grow it will be necessary for you to reflect on your everyday practice and implement appropriate changes. Childcare involves constant reviews and updates and you will need to keep on top of these in order to provide the best service possible. It takes a special person to be able to recognize that, although they may have been doing things in a certain way for many years, a different approach may be better. To be a professional you will need to build on your knowledge and resources and broaden your experiences.

Summary

At the end of this chapter you should:

- Know how to create the right image for your business.
- Be confident in deciding on the kind of service you wish to provide.
- Know how to put together a portfolio and welcome pack.
- Understand the importance of working in partnership with parents.
- Understand the importance of being a reflective practitioner.

Useful Websites

www.childminding.org
   The Scottish Childminding Association (SCMA)

www.csiw.wales.gov.uk
   Care Standards Inspectorate for Wales (CSIW)

www.ncma.org.uk
   The National Childminding Association (NCMA)

www.nicma.org
   The Northern Ireland Childminding Association (NICMA)

Getting Your Business Up and Running

5

Chapter Outline

National Standards
- Standard 1 – Suitable Person
- Standard 2 – Organization
- Standard 5 – Equipment
- Standard 6 – Safety

Units of the Diploma in Home-Based Childcare
- Unit 1 – Introduction to Childcare Practice

Making your home safe for children

It is absolutely essential that you ensure that the children in your care are safe at all times, whether they are playing indoors or outdoors or whether they are on an outing or school run. It is *your* responsibility as a childminder to ensure that the areas you have designated for the children to use are safe and free from any potential hazards; and that the toys and equipment you provide are safe and suitable for the age and stage of development of the child using them.

You must know what constitutes danger, how to avoid danger and how to reduce the risk of accidents. Obviously accidents can, and do happen even to the most diligent of childminders – and so you must also know how to deal with accidents when necessary.

In research carried out on behalf of The Royal Society for the Prevention of Accidents (RoSPA) it was found that more than 5,000 children between the ages of 0–4 years were involved in an accident in the lounge/dining/play/study areas of the home, as opposed to just over 2,000 in the kitchen. It seems therefore that, although the kitchen is probably regarded as the most dangerous room in the house, it is the rooms where children spend the majority of their time that accidents will often occur and it is for this reason that you should be extra vigilant when assessing your home and you should make sure that the children are safe in the rooms designated for them to play.

Statistics also show that a much higher percentage of boys, between the ages of 0–14 years, will suffer from accidents than girls. The research carried out makes for startling reading and I cannot stress enough how important it is that you consider very carefully which areas of your home you are intending to allow children access to and how you will ensure that these areas are completely safe for the children to use. RoSPA produce some very good literature on how to keep your home and garden safe for children and also provide relevant training.

During your registration visit and any subsequent inspections you have you will need to prove to the inspector that you have a good understanding of what constitutes danger and how you will ensure the safety of the children in your care. However, it will be your responsibility to make sure that you continue to promote a safe working environment at all times and not just when an inspector is present. It is not sufficient to simply recognize the dangers and address these when time or indeed finances are available. Budgeting for safety equipment is an essential part of your job as a childminder and it is very important that you ensure that all your equipment is checked and maintained to guarantee that it is in good working condition.

It is important to assess your home to determine where the most likely places are that an accident could happen and to try to make these places as risk free as possible.

Exercise

Make a list of any accidents that have occurred recently in your home and answer the following questions:

1 Where did the accident happen?
2 Who was involved?
3 Was the injury serious?
4 Did the injured person require hospital treatment?
5 How did you handle the situation?
6 Could the accident have been avoided?
7 What measures have you put in place to avoid a repeat accident?

The answers you give in the exercise above should help you to pinpoint the hazardous areas in your own home and make you think of ways to eliminate the risks.

A very good way of assessing risks to young children is to see potential dangers through *their* eyes. It is a good idea to get down on your knees and *crawl* around your living room to look at the area from a child's level. Did you realize that the glass vase on the window sill is easily reached by a toddler and that the flex from the table lamp is trailing in a way that could easily cause someone to trip over and fall?

Exercise

Get down on your hands and knees and crawl around your home! See things from a child's viewpoint. Make a list of the potential dangers to a child when you are looking at the room through *their* eyes.

Although the object of the next part of this chapter is to look at ways in which to avoid serious accidents in the home, it is worth remembering that it is impossible to eliminate every risk of danger. All children will suffer from the odd bump and bruise and this is all part of growing up. Children will, and indeed should, be allowed to explore their environment; however, it is up to you to ensure that while they are learning about their surroundings they are not subjected to unnecessary dangers.

In order to make a thorough check of your property and eliminate potential hazards, it is important to look at each room individually.

The kitchen

This is probably the most dangerous place in the house for young children. They will be completely unaware of the potential hazards, which are numerous in this particular room. It is essential to take into account your *own* kitchen, its layout and the equipment within but you should consider the following:

1	Ovens	Oven doors must be shut at all times.
		Children must not be allowed to touch hot surfaces.
2	Hobs	Pan handles must face inwards.
		Tea towels, oven gloves, etc. must not be allowed to trail over the hob or cooker.
		Children must not be allowed to put anything on top of the cooker even when it is turned off, nor must they be allowed to touch the hob.
3	Fridge/Freezers	Doors must be securely shut at all times; if possible use a door lock.
4	Washing Machines	Doors must be securely shut at all times; if possible use a door lock.
5	Tumble Driers	Ensure that the doors are shut at all times.

6	Hot Objects	Pans must not be left on a work surface with handles faced out, nor must they be accessible to children.
7	Cleaning Materials	Must be kept in their original containers in a locked cupboard .
8	Medicine	All medicine should be stored in a locked cupboard out of the reach of children.
		If medicine needs to be stored in a fridge, fit a suitable lock.
9	Alcohol	Must be stored out of the reach of children or in a locked cupboard.
10	Plastic bags	Stored out of the sight or reach of children.
11	Knives	Should be stored in a secure cupboard and must never be left on work surfaces.
12	Kettles	Ensure these are pushed to the back of work surfaces out of the reach of children.
		Flexes must not be left dangling over the edge of work surfaces nor must they trail near a hob.
13	Electrical Equipment	All microwaves, irons, toasters, etc. should be stored out of the reach of children and the flexes to these electrical appliances must not be accessible to children.

Figure 5.1 Hazards in the kitchen

> **Remember**
>
> The kitchen is probably the most dangerous room in the house. The potential hazards are numerous and it is vital that children are adequately supervised at all times.

The living room/playroom

The living room and playroom are probably the rooms where you will spend most of your time when childminding and it is essential that these rooms are completely free of any potential hazards. The children must be safe to play in these rooms without coming to any harm, and they should therefore be as child-friendly as possible.

1	Ornaments	Keep all ornaments and small objects to a minimum and out of the reach of children.
2	Floor Space	Ensure that the floor area is as clutter free as possible. Encourage children to put things away before getting other toys out.
3	Hot Drinks	Hot drinks must never be left in a child's reach. Do not place hot drinks on coffee tables.
4	Storage	Children's toys should be stored sensibly; they should be easily accessible without the need for the child to climb to reach them. Fix shelving securely to the wall
5	Plants	These must be placed out of the reach of children and should not pose a threat to health.
6	Cigarettes	Childminders must not smoke while they have children in their care. Cigarettes, lighters and matches should be kept in a locked cupboard out of the reach of children.
7	Fires	It is essential that a firmly fixed fireguard is in place around the *whole* of the fire place at all times. Your home must be fitted with smoke alarms and you must check these regularly. It is also important that you have a fire blanket and a fire extinguisher in your home and that you know how and when to use them.
8	TVs, Videos, DVDs, etc.	Always ensure that the flexes to all electrical items are not left trailing. Fit guards to video recorders.
9	Toys	Check toys and equipment regularly for broken pieces, missing parts or sharp edges and ensure that items are either repaired or replaced as necessary.

Case Study 4

Cathy cares for two children aged 6 and 8 before and after school. She also looks after a 10 month old baby full time. In the school holidays Cathy agrees to care for the older children for three days of the week. The older children are complaining because they want to get the Lego bricks out and Cathy is concerned about the choking hazard to the baby, who is at the crawling stage. Cathy explains that the baby could choke on the small Lego bricks and tells the older children that they can have the Lego out when the baby goes down for his afternoon sleep. In the meantime Cathy allows all the children to play with the chunkier duplo bricks. The children appear to be happy with this solution.

1 Do you think that Cathy was right to refuse the older children the Lego bricks?
2 What must Cathy make sure she does when the baby is asleep?
3 What else could have been done in this situation?

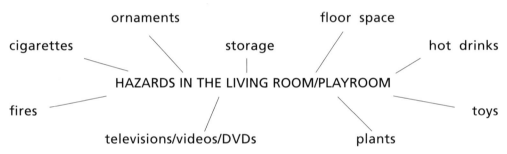

Figure 5.2 Hazards in the living room/playroom

The dining room

1	Tables	Ensure that objects placed on the tables are not near the edge and that table cloths do not hang over making it possible for small children to pull objects onto themselves.
2	Seating	Provide suitable seating for every child, i.e. booster seats or high chairs with safety harnesses.
3	Crockery/cutlery	Ensure that children are supplied with crockery and cutlery appropriate to their age and stage of development. Teach children the correct way to use cutlery and do not allow them to play with knives and forks.
4	Feeding Bottles	Never leave a baby alone with a bottle or propped up to feed.

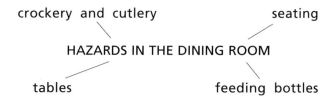

Figure 5.3 Hazards in the dining room

> ### Remember
> Children should be encouraged to sit at the table while eating and drinking and should not be allowed to wander around. Children should never be left unattended during meal times or when hot food and drink is being served.

Sleeping areas

1	Pillows	NEVER use pillows for children under the age of 18 months.
2	Beds/cots	Ensure that your beds and cots conform to legal requirements, mattresses should fit snugly and meet safety standards.
		Never put young children into a top bunk.
		Avoid cots with sides that slide down unless they have secure fastenings that are child friendly.
		Take care when deciding whether to fit bed guards as these can encourage children to climb.
		Use clean sheets and bedding for each child.
3	Supervision	Children must be supervised at all times.

Figure 5.4 Hazards in sleeping areas

The bathroom and toilet

1 Water   Hot water should be available for washing at all times and should not exceed 54°C.

Always run cold water into a bath first before adding hot.

2 Medicines   Medicines should be stored in a locked cabinet out of the reach of children.

3 Cleaning Materials All cleaning materials, air fresheners and disinfectants should be stored in their original packaging and out of the reach of children.

4 Potties/Toilet Seats Ensure that these are not cracked or split.

Provide a suitable step for young children to reach the toilet safely.

5 Supervision   Young children should be supervised in the toilet or bathroom.

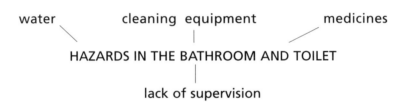

Figure 5.5 Hazards in bathroom and toilet

> ### Remember
>
> Young children should always be supervised while using the bathroom, however, it is important to take into account the child's age and need for privacy when deciding how much supervision is required.

The hall and stairs

1 Safety Gates   Must conform to BS 4125 Standards.

Must be firmly fixed in place to both the top and bottom of the stairs.

Avoid gates which do not open and have to be climbed over as these can be very dangerous.

2 Space   Children should not be allowed to play on the stairs.

Keep stairs free of clutter at all times.

3 Carpets   Replace any frayed, worn or loose carpets.

4 Banisters   Do not allow children to swing on banisters and balustrades.

5 Windows   Never place objects or items of furniture under windows that a child can climb on.

6 Lighting   Ensure that your hall and stairs are well lit at all times.

Figure 5.6 Hazards in the hall and on the stairs

Every home is of course different and it is important that you look carefully at your *own* home and its contents and identify which areas need to be addressed. You must look at your premises with a critical eye and never ignore areas which may prove potential hazards. You must realize that it is not simply sufficient to carry out a risk assessment on your home once, prior to registration, but that this is a continual necessary requirement which you must perform periodically.

Even after diligently checking your home and conforming to all the necessary regulations it is still not possible to guarantee that an accident will not happen. The most important thing to remember and the one thing that will *always* reduce the risk of an accident is to ensure that you adequately supervise the children in your care at all times.

> ### Exercise
> Carry out a risk assessment on each room in your home and list any potential hazards. Next make a list of any changes or improvements you feel are necessary to minimize these potential dangers.

Making your garden safe for children

Young children should not be allowed to play outdoors alone. They should be in your sight and hearing at all times.

It is a good idea to look at your own garden critically before deciding on the best course of action to take. You may be lucky enough to have a huge garden which you consider to be a haven for children to explore. However, if it is fraught with potential dangers then you will have to look at practical ways of making the area safe. This could mean fencing off a particular area which you intend to designate solely for your childminding business. By keeping a special area for the children to play in you can ensure it is safe from any potential dangers and it will allow you the freedom to plan an outdoor area especially for children. If you have young children of your own it is probably true to say that your garden will be a reasonably safe place to play as you will no doubt be allowing your own children access to it. However, have you thought about the following potential dangers?

Potential hazards to consider in your garden are:

1	Ponds	Must be fenced off and access completely prohibited.
2	Drains	Must be fitted with suitable covers.
3	Dustbins	Access must be prohibited at all times to dustbins, compost heaps, etc.
4	Swings/Slides	Regular checks must be made for wear and tear. Large items should be securely fastened to the ground to avoid tipping and suitable mats or wood chippings must be used underneath to ensure that children are not exposed to hard surfaces should they fall.
5	Washing Lines	Must not be strung across the children's play area. Rotary washing lines must be removed or adequately covered to prevent children becoming entangled in them.
6	Plants	Gardens should be free from any trees or plants which pose a danger to children.
7	Pets	Must be exercised away from play areas.
8	Tools	Must be securely locked away.
9	Greenhouses	Must be fenced off or be fitted with protective film.
10	Bicycles	Must be adequately maintained.

Figure 5.7 Hazards in the garden

Exercise

Carry out a risk assessment of your garden. List any potential hazards and the action you will take to minimize any risks to children.

Poisonous plants and trees

The following is a list of some of the more common plants and trees which should be avoided when considering which plants are suitable for a garden to be used by young children. If your garden has any of these plants or trees you must remove them or fence them off to restrict access by children:

- Angels Trumpets
- Autumn Crocus
- Castor Oil Plant
- Daffodil bulbs
- Daphne
- Deadly Nightshade
- Foxglove
- Glory Lily
- Hellebore
- Hemlock
- Hyacinth
- Ivy
- Laburnum
- Lantana
- Leopard Lily
- Lily Of The Valley
- Monkshood
- Oleander
- Poinsettia
- Poison Primrose
- Rhubarb leaves
- Rue
- Spurge
- The Poisonous Primula
- Thorn apple
- Wild Arum
- Winter Cherry
- Woody Nightshade
- Yew

In addition to poisonous plants and trees which can cause harm to children it is also advisable to avoid planting anything with unusual or colourful berries which may prove a temptation to young children. Nettles and thistles should also be removed to prevent stings and scratches.

The most common symptoms suffered after contact with a poisonous plant are:

- Diarrhoea
- Dizziness
- Vomiting
- Drowsiness
- Blistering of the skin
- Itchy rashes

If a child in your care experiences any of these symptoms after coming in contact with poisonous plants you should consult a doctor immediately.

Toys and equipment

As with any new business you will need to purchase equipment. Childminders who are already parents themselves may have a lot of the basic equipment and many toys that can be used. If this is the case it may just be necessary for you to ensure that the equipment you do have is safe and in a good state of repair, and then recognize which other items you will need to buy to add to your existing equipment.

Choosing suitable toys

Despite strict regulations for the manufacture of toys and equipment, it is still possible to buy cheap imitations which are both illegal and unsafe and you must be careful to avoid these at all costs. Take particular care if you are purchasing toys from car boot sales, jumble sales, etc. and always look for the necessary safety symbols.

It is a good idea to get into the habit of checking all your purchases of toys and equipment for one of the symbols or logos which guarantee that the goods conform to British Safety Standards.

Some items may have a 'BS' number while others will have the letters CE or the kite or lion mark, as illustrated below. Symbols which show a child's face and age group show that the toys are *unsuitable* for a child between the ages stated.

Exercise

Familiarize yourself with the safety symbols below and get into the habit of checking that all the toys and equipment you purchase for your childminding business conform to these standards.

Figure 5.8 Safety symbols to look for on toys

Choosing suitable equipment

Baby Walkers
I would never advise anyone to purchase a baby walker. They can be a very dangerous piece of equipment and evidence has shown that baby walkers can actually hinder a child's development. Childminders are discouraged from using this piece of equipment.

High Chairs
High chairs should be sturdy and placed on a flat surface. Table-mounted high chairs are not considered sufficiently stable and should be avoided. Children should never be left in a high chair unsupervised, and high chairs must always be fitted with suitable harnesses which should be adjusted to fit the size of each individual child using the chair.

Baby Seats
Baby seats should always be placed on a flat sturdy surface and never on a table or work surface. Harnesses must be fitted and adjusted to suit the individual child.

Safety Gates

Safety gates should be fitted to both the top and bottom of the stairs. You should avoid purchasing gates which do not open and require you to step over them as these can be extremely dangerous, particularly at the top of a flight of stairs. Although safety gates are essential for stairs they are equally useful to prevent children from gaining access to other rooms which may pose dangers, such as the kitchen.

Locks

It is advisable to use window locks in the rooms which the children in your care will have access to.

Prams and Buggies

It is essential that you check and regularly maintain your prams and buggies. Check for wear and tear and broken pieces and repair or replace whenever necessary. Always use a suitable harness which can be adjusted to suit the child using it. You may find that the parents of a child you are caring for will offer to provide a pram or buggy for you to use and, if this is the case, it is just as important for you to check these for wear and tear as you would your own equipment. If you feel that the item is a danger to the child you must notify the parent immediately and refrain from using it. If you are caring for two young children who are not at an adequate walking stage you must provide a double buggy or other suitable method of transporting the children, e.g. a baby sling. Never be tempted to fit two children into a single buggy even for a short journey.

Cots and Beds

Mattresses should fit the cot or bed snugly and conform to British Safety Standards. Travel cots are sufficient for the purpose of childminding but if you do opt to purchase a cot with sides that slide down it is essential that these have secure childproof fastenings. Although bed guards may be considered beneficial by some to prevent young children from falling out of bed, it is worth considering the implications that these guards may have for children who view them as potential climbing frame. Pillows should not be used for children under the age of 18 months and if you have a bunk bed you must not allow young children to use the top bunk.

Potties and Toilet Seats

It is possible to purchase toilet seats which are designed to fit over a standard adult seat and if you choose to buy one of these you must ensure that the seat fits firmly and that you supply a secure step for the child to reach the seat without having to climb or pull themselves up. Potties and toilet seats are usually made of plastic and you should check these regularly for splits or cracks and replace them whenever necessary.

When deciding which toys and equipment you are going to purchase you must first decide on the age of the children you are hoping to provide care for. Obviously the items you will need to purchase for a 12-month-old baby will differ tremendously from those needed to care for a seven-year-old child attending school.

Basic Equipment for Babies and Toddlers

- A cot and new mattress – it may be sufficient to provide a travel cot
- Sheets and blankets
- High chair with fitted harness
- Car seats
- Pushchair – you may require a double buggy if you are caring for two young children
- Potty and training seat
- Changing mat
- Bibs, bottles, plastic bowls, plates, cups and cutlery
- Appropriate safety equipment such as:
  - harnesses
  - stair gates
  - fireguard
  - smoke alarms
  - cupboard locks
  - window locks
  - drain covers

Basic Toys for Babies and Toddlers

- A good selection of clean rattles and teething rings
- A selection of clean soft toys
- A variety of stimulating toys such as stacking bricks, shape sorters, etc.
- Simple games and puzzles
- A good selection of books. It is a good idea to provide fabric books and books with both paper and cardboard pages to appeal to the very young.
- A variety of collage materials, paper, crayons and paints
- Dressing-up clothes and props for role-play
- A 'treasure basket' – a very simple idea to encourage babies and young children to explore and stimulate all their senses. Fill a small basket, box or container with *safe* objects found around the house. Choose things which have interesting shapes or textures such as a wooden clothes peg, a small baby mirror, a pumice stone, clean vegetables, an orange, a wooden cotton reel, a fir cone, etc. It is very important that you ensure that the objects are not dangerous and that they do not have any sharp edges. All objects should be of a suitable size so that they can not be inserted into the ears or nose nor can they be swallowed. Do not leave a baby alone with the treasure basket but watch from a little distance in order that the baby or toddler can explore the basket themselves.
- Outdoor toys such as balls, hoops, skittles, ride-on toys, etc.

> **Remember**
>
> It is very important that you provide a range of toys and materials which are stimulating and interesting. Your resources should be appropriate to the age and development of the children you are caring for and must promote equality of opportunity. These requirements are necessary for you to meet Standard 5 of the National Standards – Equipment.

Basic Equipment for Pre-School Children

- A cot or bed depending on the age and size of the child
- A suitable pushchair
- Reins and harnesses
- Safety equipment as listed above

Basic Toys for Pre-School Children

- A good selection of books. Try to provide both fiction and non-fiction books which have lots of pictures or photographs
- Dressing-up clothes and props for role-play such as toy food and cooking utensils
- Paper, paints, crayons and collage materials
- Duplo, Lego and other building materials
- Musical instruments
- Games
- Jigsaw puzzles
- Play-Doh and modelling equipment
- Educational videos and music tapes
- Outdoor toys such as balls, skittles, hoops, skipping ropes, etc.

Basic Equipment for School-Aged Children

- A quiet area with a comfortable table and chair for them to complete any homework tasks.

Basic Toys for School-Aged Children

- All of the items listed for pre-school children could also be used for younger school-aged children.
- Additional games for older children such as Monopoly, Scrabble, Ludo, playing cards, etc. can be supplied.
- A selection of books covering both fiction and non-fiction topics. Try to supply books with fewer pictures for older children.
- Outdoor toys such as balls, skittles, hoops, skipping ropes, etc.

The above lists are by no means complete and you may think of many other items which you could include. If you have children of your own and already have a large selection of toys it may be worth considering purchasing more 'select' play equipment to appeal to parents, and in particular their children. For example, a ball pool or play house. These items can be costly but if you already have lots of basic equipment which is still in good order you may have the funds to purchase one really good piece of equipment which will appeal to a wide range of ages. You cannot be expected to have *all* the toys and equipment to suit the needs of *every* child you may encounter so it is important to recognize which toys are essential and which are an added bonus or luxury. Ensure you have the essential toys and equipment which will appeal to the widest range of children and then add to your resources as and when finances allow.

Exercise

Make a list of the basic equipment you already have, then add to the list the toys and equipment you feel you need to purchase initially. Secondly, make a separate 'wish list' and put all the items you would like to purchase within say a two year period, as and when finances allow. Keep this list handy and revise it periodically when you take on any new children.

Working with another childminder or assistant

The majority of childminders work alone, however, there are a large number of child-minders who opt to work together with a co-childminder or employ an assistant. There are both advantages and disadvantages to employing an assistant or choosing to work with another registered childminder and we will look at these now:

Advantages

- There is someone to share the workload with
- You will be allowed to care for more children
- New ideas and views are brought to the business
- There is someone to talk to in times of crisis or to talk through a difficult situation with
- Children will benefit from extra adult contact
- It prevents childminders from becoming lonely and introduces other adult company to the business
- It gives added flexibility and backup in times of illness and holidays
- There is someone on hand in times of emergencies
- The costs involved in setting up your business and providing the necessary toys and equipment can be shared.

> **Remember**
>
> Working with another childminder or an assistant directly relates to Standard 1 of the National Standards – Suitable Person – and you will be expected to show an Ofsted inspector your procedures for employing an assistant or working with a co-childminder.

Disadvantages

- It may be difficult to ascertain who is the boss
- You may find it hard to give clear instructions
- You will have to decide whose house the childminding business is to be run from
- You will need to work out who will be responsible for certain duties
- The childminder whose home is being used may resent the intrusion on their property when their co-worker appears to have no similar inconveniences
- Friendships may be stretched if you find yourself spending long hours together
- You may not both have the same goals in mind
- One of you may be more committed to the business than the other
- It may be difficult to decide which person is going to attend training courses.

> **Remember**
>
> If you decide to employ an assistant you will be expected to show an Ofsted inspector how you supervise their work, including your methods for giving instructions and supporting and guiding the assistant in their work – this information relates directly to Standard 2 – Organization.

Case Study 5

Carol and Alana have decided to work together as childminders. It has been agreed that they will work from Carol's house as this is the larger of the two and more suitable for running a business from. Carol has never been a particularly organized person and is daunted by the prospect of keeping accounts, negotiating contracts and writing policies. Alana is confident in these areas of childminding but is not a particularly creative person. The two talk through the potential difficulties and agree which person will be responsible for which roles. Carol agrees to plan the activities and outings for the children, while Alana is given the responsibility for the paperwork and bookkeeping.

1 Do you think Carol and Alana have found a sensible solution?
2 What problems may occur with this arrangement?
3 What would you do differently?

If you do decide to work with another childminder you must agree, from the outset, who will be responsible for what and draw up a plan together which clearly outlines what can be expected from each of you. Never leave the business side of things to chance as it is vital that you know exactly who is responsible for what when it comes to the smooth running of the business. This may be very easy to ascertain if, for example, one of you is very artistic and the other is a good organizer. It makes sense that the artistic person should be in charge of the activities, while the organized person is responsible for keeping the accounts and books up-to-date.

If you decide to work with another person but are not entirely happy with a 'partnership' then you may like to consider employing an assistant to help. You may only require additional help at certain times of the day, say before and after school, or on the days of the week when you are most busy. An assistant does not need to be registered as a childminder, however they do need to be checked by the Criminal Records Bureau to ensure their suitability to work with children. You will also need to obtain written permission from the parents of any children you provide care for that they have no objection to you working with an assistant.

If you do decide to employ an assistant rather than work with another childminder as a partnership, then you will be responsible for Income Tax and National Insurance payments for your employee and it is important that you comply with the employment law in this case. You will be expected to pay your assistant the minimum wage and, as an employer, you will also need to have employer's liability insurance in addition to public liability insurance, which is mandatory for all childminding practices.

Exercise

If you are considering working with a friend, either as a co-childminder or as an employer, consider carefully all the implications this may have for your business. Make a list of the pros and cons for working with a partner against those of working with an employee and decide which option would suit you the best.

Summary

At the end of this chapter you should:

- Understand the importance of ensuring that children in your care are safe at all times.
- Be able to identify hazards in the home and garden.
- Understand how to minimize hazards in the home and garden.
- Be confident in choosing suitable toys and equipment for the children in your care.
- Be able to decide whether you wish to work alone, with another childminder or employ an assistant; and be aware of the implications of each choice.

References

Research statistics carried out on behalf of the Royal Society for the Prevention of Accidents were taken from the 2002 Hass and Lass data: location of accident within the home by age.

Useful Websites

www.capt.org.uk
Child Accident Prevention Trust (CAPT)

www.hse.gov.uk
Health and Safety government website

www.natll.org.uk
National Association of Toy and Leisure Libraries

www.ofsted.gov.uk
Office for Standards in Education (Ofsted)

www.rospa.com
Royal Society for the Prevention of Accidents (RoSPA)

Often safety equipment and toys can be borrowed for a nominal charge from your local support group. Other useful places to order resources are:

www.elc.co.uk
Early Learning Centre

www.mothercare.co.uk
Mothercare

www.rospa.com
Royal Society for the Prevention of Accidents (RoSPA)

6

Launching Your Business

National Standards
- Standard 12 – Working in Partnership with Parents and Carers

Units of the Diploma in Home-Based Childcare
- Unit 1 – Introduction to Childcare Practice (Home-based)
- Unit 3 – The Childcare Practitioner in the Home-based Setting
- Unit 4 – Working in Partnership with Parents in the Home-based Setting

How to advertise your service

Newly qualified childminders often find themselves in the position of needing to find business and will initially need to advertise their services. Childminders who have been registered for some time may well be in the enviable position of having all their places full with, perhaps, even a waiting list. However, it is important to remember that we have all had to work at securing custom from time to time and, in order for your childminding business to thrive and make a profit, it is important that your places *remain* full. It may be possible for you to anticipate when a vacancy is likely to arise, for example when a child leaves your care to start school and, in cases such as this, you will usually have a few months' notice in order to fill your vacancy. However, there are also situations which are out of your control and which may result in one or more vacancies arising with very little notice, for example a parent facing redundancy or a disagreement which results in the termination of a contract. Depending on the nature of the termination, you will probably have only four weeks' notice, maybe less, and you must consider how you will fill your vacancy as quickly as possible.

Remember

Unit 1 of the Diploma in Home-based Childcare covers the effective marketing of a childcare business.

Waiting lists

It is a good idea to keep a record of any enquiries you receive through the course of your childminding work, regardless of whether you have a vacancy at that time or not. You may find yourself getting enquiries often and, although you may not have an immediate vacancy, it is a good idea to explain to the person making the enquiry that your places are full at present but if they would like to leave their details you will contact them if any vacancies should arise in the near future. If the enquirer is very keen to secure a place they will be pleased if the opportunity is offered to them at a later date. By taking details you have the added benefit of amassing a list of potential customers who may still require a place should the opportunity arise later.

Word of mouth

Getting yourself known in your local community is by far one of the best ways of creating business as a childminder. People who are using your service, or indeed those who have used your service, are usually happy to recommend you to other people. In addition to it being an excellent compliment, being recommended is also one of the cheapest methods of advertising you will encounter.

Notices and leaflets

Putting a card or poster in shop windows, doctors' and dentists' waiting rooms, libraries and on school noticeboards is a good way of advertising your business. So, too, is posting leaflets through letterboxes. Target local family homes. Perhaps there is a new housing development nearby. Families who are new to the area will often welcome any information regarding childcare and, if you get there first with details of your childminding service, and create a good impression, you may well secure their business immediately.

If you are intending to design posters or leaflets make sure that they look *professional*. Grubby, illegible material littered with spelling mistakes will not create the impression you are hoping for and will have an adverse effect on your business. A simple, eye-catching design, similar to the one below, is recommended, and remember *never* to put your full address on any advertising material. A telephone number should suffice and, upon receiving enquiries, only give out your address to serious callers wishing to make an appointment to visit.

> # REGISTERED CHILDMINDER
> *Has full- and part-time vacancies*
>
> **Newly registered with Ofsted**
>
> **First-aid trained**
>
> **References available**
>
> **Local school and playgroup drop-offs and collections**
>
> **School holiday cover available**
>
> **Competitive rates**
>
> ☆ ☆ ☆ ☺ ☆ ☆ ☆
>
> For further details and to make an
> appointment to visit please contact . . .

Figure 6.1 Sample advertising card or poster

Children's information service

Your local Children's Information Service office will keep a list of registered childminders in your area. They are responsible for furnishing parents and carers with details of childminders and, with your permission, will add your details to their Internet files.

Signs

If you live on a busy street, a sign placed in a prominent position in your window may be an effective method of advertising. As with posters and leaflets, the sign should look professional and be clear and legible. A consideration here is whether or not you want to attract attention to the fact that you are caring for children on your premises. A notice placed in your car may also be a good way of advertising your business, getting your name about while you are driving around your local area.

Childminding groups

Attending support groups regularly with other childminders is an invaluable way of getting yourself and your business known. Fellow childminders who are unable to offer a place to someone making enquires are often willing to pass on the names and contact details of others. Likewise you may be able to help out other childminders should you not have a vacancy at any particular time. Some areas also have childminding coordinators and it is a good idea to enquire whether there is someone in your area with this responsibility and, if so, inform them of your vacancies.

Newspapers

I would offer a word of caution before rushing in to advertise your childminding business in the local press. In my own experience this method has not proved a great success and, with the numerous other ways of advertising your business, I would advise that you leave newspapers as a last resort. For one thing, advertisements can be expensive, and for another they can often attract unwanted responses. If you do decide to advertise in a newspaper, keep the advert short and to the point and, as with leaflets and posters, *never* give your full address.

Telephone directories

Childminders should be able to place a free line advertisement in the Yellow Pages or the Thomson Local. This has proved a very effective method of advertising for many childminders, however, like newspapers, these advertisements can attract unwanted junk mail and unsolicited telephone calls offering business services so, once again, proceed with caution.

To enquire about the possibility of a free line advertisement contact:

Yellow Pages on 0808 100 8182

Thomson Local on 01252 555 555

When promoting your childminding business, always bear in mind the following points:

- When producing postcards, leaflets or posters always make sure they contain all the relevant information a parent may need, have no punctuation, grammar or spelling mistakes and are clear and easy to understand.
- Try to produce your postcards, leaflets or posters using a computer – they look far more professional. If you don't have access to a computer, ask a friend or make use of your local library or community centre resources. Failing this, consider using the services of a print shop.
- Never use photographs of the children you are caring for in your promotional material unless you have prior written permission from their parents and never print their names.

Nannies

In addition to using some of the above methods such as producing leaflets and putting advertisements in newspapers, nannies also have the added benefit of being able to advertise their services with a recruitment agency. It may be worth considering Internet childcare recruitment sites such as www.nannyjob.co.uk.

Interviewing potential customers

Although you may not realize it at the time, the first 'interview' you have with potential customers is when you take their initial enquiry. This may be face-to-face in the playground or over the telephone while you are working. The enquiry may be already arranged, for example, through a friend, or take you completely by surprise. Whatever the situation you must be prepared. Always remember that you are a professional person offering a professional service. It will not help if you are caught off guard and appear flustered and inexperienced. If you are new to childminding and have all your places to fill, interviewing potential customers can be daunting and you may find yourself trying too hard to please. It is a good idea to have a well-rehearsed dialogue in place so that you know what to say when you receive an enquiry and appear confident and efficient. The following points should be incorporated in any conversations you have with potential customers:

1 If someone calls at a bad time – perhaps you are feeding a baby or changing a nappy – explain the situation and offer to call them back. This will enable you to give the enquiry your full attention.

2 Always appear interested in the enquirer and listen carefully to what they have to say. Even if you do not have a vacancy, it is worth taking a note of their details in case you have availability at a future date.

3 Stick to the basics in order to ascertain what the parent is looking for; the number of days or hours required, number of childcare places needed, etc.

4 Give a short account about yourself. Include the number of years you have been childminding and mention your qualifications to date. If you are newly qualified, focus on your best selling points, what you have to offer and any features you may have, such as a large playroom or outdoor playground facilities.

5 Ask questions about the child. Show you are genuinely interested in the child and try to build on what the parent is telling you. For example, if the parent works shift patterns and you are willing to offer this kind of flexibility, tell them. If they mention that their child requires a special diet and you are able to meet this request, inform them. The parent needs to feel that *you* are their ideal childminder from the outset and it is up to you to prove them right!

When you have ascertained whether or not you have a suitable vacancy then you will need to arrange a time for the parent to visit you so you can meet face-to-face. Some people prefer to call when you are working so that they can see for themselves the kind or service you provide and the environment you work in when the children are present. Others prefer to call in an evening, perhaps after they have finished work, or at the weekend. You must decide together which is the most suitable time for the appointment. A lot of childminders prefer to make two appointments: one for the parents to get a 'feel' for the setting and witness you working first hand, and then, if they feel they would like to agree terms and negotiate a contract, a second appointment is made, without any children present in order to minimize the distractions, while the appropriate paperwork is completed, and the policies and procedures are explained.

When you first meet up with parents it is important to make a good impression. You will probably have already spoken to them on the telephone and should, from the information they have already supplied, have a good idea of what the parents are looking for with regard to childcare.

Before you welcome the parents into your home, scrutinize your childminding setting. Look at your home from the perspective of a first-time visitor and ask yourself if it gives the right impression. If there are no children present, your home should be tidy and free from toys cluttering the floor. If there are children present it is important that you choose suitable activities to keep them amused and entertained while you speak to the parents. Whether there are children present or not, your home must be clean and presentable.

Exercise

Think of the words which most parents would use to describe the kind of childcare setting they would ideally like to find for their child. Look at your own home carefully and write down the words which you feel adequately describe your environment. Compare these words.

It is probably true to say that most people would, when asked, describe the ideal childcare setting for their child to be:

- Safe
- Welcoming
- Happy
- Homely
- Enjoyable
- Educational
- Loving
- Stimulating
- Fun

You have the difficult task of trying to convey as many of the positive things a parent is looking for into a short interview. Try to plan ahead and prepare yourself for the possible questions they may ask, and have your portfolio ready to show.

In addition to ensuring that your home looks presentable and that you have prepared your portfolio, it is of course essential that you yourself look the part. Dress for the situation. Just as dirty, scruffy or inappropriate clothing will make the wrong impression, parents will not expect to see you dressed in a business suit and high heels. Aim to look professional while bearing in mind that you work with children.

Make sure that your body language doesn't let you down. Avoid mumbling, folding arms and looking at the ground. Your body language can say as much as your words so it is essential that you make eye contact, smile and above all listen to what is being said and show interest!

The interview is very important. This is the initial meeting when parents will either take to you or not. They will probably make their minds up early on in the meeting and it is vital that you sell yourself and your service to the best of your ability. Try to avoid any negative comments and if an answer you give results in an unimpressed response, act quickly and try to turn the situation around. Some parents, for example, may be unhappy at their child having to do the school run each day. Try to explain that this trip is turned into an enjoyable experience by stopping off at the park, feeding the ducks or visiting the library. Explain that by introducing school life early on their child will get used to the setting and become familiar with the teachers and children so that when they start themselves they may not be as overwhelmed as they would be if they had never been in the environment.

Case Study 6

Brenda arranged an interview with Bob and Lena with a view to offering a childcare place to their son, three-year-old Lenny. Brenda spoke to Lena on the telephone and understood that the placement would be for three days per week: Monday, Tuesday and Friday. Brenda had a vacancy on these days and arranged for the parents to call at her home so they could discuss childcare.

When Bob and Lena arrived with Lenny, Brenda showed them into her living room. Lenny wasn't interested in any of the toys Brenda had got out for him, preferring to use the sofa as a trampoline. When Brenda politely asked Lenny not to jump on the furniture, his dad laughed and explained that he does that 'all the time at home'. The interview seemed to go from bad to worse and Brenda found the parents uncommunicative and difficult. The days they had initially asked for had been changed and Brenda felt that she was unable to work with the parents and offer the childcare they were looking for. Brenda politely explained that she did not have vacancies on the days they were now asking for and suggested that Bob and Lena try alternative childminders.

1 In your opinion, did Brenda handle this situation well?
2 How could Brenda have handled the problem with Lenny jumping on her furniture?
3 How could Brenda have avoided the problem with regard to the change of days requested?

It is important to remember that not everyone you arrange an interview with will take up a childcare place with you and, in fact, you may not wish to care for the child yourself after having spoken in depth to the parents. The interview is as much a deciding factor for you as it is for the parents and the child. You may think the child is adorable but if you think you will have difficulty relating to the parents, or if the parents are requesting things you are not happy or confident providing then the interview is the time when you will realize these differences. It is very important that you do not promise anything that you will have difficulty providing in order to secure business. If the parents need you to work until 7pm and you know this is not possible with your own family commitments, it is important that you are honest in order that a compromise can be found or an alternative childminder sought. Problems will not go away once a contract is signed – they will increase and cause resentment.

When you are attempting to 'sell' your business to prospective parents, remember that childminding offers a unique childcare opportunity and you should concentrate on the positive things you have to offer, such as:

- **A high adult:child ratio.** In comparison with nursery settings, childminders have only a small number of children to care for and are therefore able to provide the time, attention, stimulation and love that all the children require.
- **Continuity of care.** Often childminders are able to offer childcare from when a child is only a few months old, right through to their teens.
- **Home from home environment.** Many parents choose childminders because they like the idea of their children being cared for in an environment similar to the one they experience at home. They are looking for someone who will encourage their child to take part in everyday tasks such as shopping and cooking and are happy for them to become a part of their local community.
- **Flexible childcare.** Unlike nurseries, childminders offer the flexibility of early morning, evening, overnight or weekend care and are especially helpful to parents who work shift patterns.
- **Tailored service.** Childminders are able to offer a personal service tailored to each individual child's needs. Whether a child needs help with their homework, assistance in learning to read or encouragement to use the potty, a childminder is able to offer the right support at the right time.

Settling a child into your setting

Ideally you should have the opportunity to get to know a child over a period of time. You should arrange with the child's parents for them to allow the child to spend a series of short sessions with you so that you can get to know one another before the parent has to leave them for any lengthy periods of time. If this is possible then I would suggest that the child is left for perhaps an hour, initially, building up to maybe two or three hours over a period of several weeks.

If you have agreed to take on a young baby it may be that the mother is still on maternity leave and this provides a great opportunity for you to settle the baby into your care over a period of perhaps 4–6 weeks. Try to incorporate feeds into your settling-in times so that you and the mother can be sure that the baby will take bottles from you.

Of course, it is not always possible to settle children in over a period of weeks and there may be times when it is necessary for you to take a child on at short notice. In these cases try to get as much information about the child as possible, ask about their likes and dislikes and work with the parent to ensure that the child settles into your setting with as little disruption as possible.

All children are different and, while some cope admirably when separated from their parents, others find the transition difficult and may take several weeks or even months to settle. There are a number of ways in which you can help a child who is experiencing difficulty settling:

1 Whenever possible, arrange for short, regular visits to your home prior to the start of the placement.
2 Encourage the parent to stay with the child while they are in your setting and allow the child to witness the friendship you have with their parent in order for you to establish their trust and feel welcome and secure.
3 If possible, visit the child in their own home. Children who feel insecure in another setting are often completely at ease in their own home and it may be the challenges that the setting has to offer, rather than you as the carer that may be unsettling. By gaining the child's trust on their own territory you may be able to eliminate any anxiety.
4 Arrange for the child to bring one or two special toys, a comforter or dummy to your setting so that they have familiar things around them.

Figure 6.1

Exercise

Think of ways in which you can help a child to settle into your childminding setting. What types of games and activities could you use to help a child feel welcome and secure?

When the time comes for the parent to leave their child, encourage them to do so as quickly as possible, but without 'sneaking off'. Long, drawn-out farewells can be stressful to children but, by sneaking away while a child is distracted, parents could inadvertently be encouraging insecurity and distrust.

Reassure the child once their parent has left, tell them they will be back for them soon but in the meantime you have lots of activities available. Spend as much time with the new child as possible and try to provide the kind of activities or games you know they will like (prior consultation with a parent is always a good idea).

Summary

At the end of this chapter you should:

- Know how and where to advertise your business.
- Be able to prepare a satisfactory advert offering your services.
- Be confident conducting interviews with potential customers.
- Understand the differing needs of children who are new to your setting and be knowledgeable in settling children in with the minimum of upset and disruption.

Useful Websites

www.childminding.org
The Scottish Childminding Association (SCMA)

www.csiw.wales.gov.uk
Care Standards Inspectorate for Wales (CSIW)

www.ncma.org.uk
The National Childminding Association (NCMA)

www.nicma.org
The Northern Ireland Childminding Association (NICMA)

7 Negotiating a Contract

National Standards
- Standard 12 – Working in Partnership with Parents
- Standard 14 – Documentation

Units of the Diploma in Home-based Childcare
- Unit 3 – The Childcare Practitioner in the Home-based Setting
- Unit 4 – Working in Partnership with Parents in the Home-based Setting

Setting fees

Unlike other childcare practitioners such as nannies, childminders are not actually employed by the person whose children they are caring for. Childminders are self-employed and as such have the flexibility to set their own working hours and rates of pay. Although you must remember to be competitive when setting your rates, the amount you charge is largely down to your own discretion, but you may like to take several things into consideration when setting your fees, such as:

- The hours you are prepared to work
- The qualifications and experience you have gained
- The service you provide (some childminders provide a collection and drop-off service and if this is the case you should consider the costs you incur for petrol, insurance, etc.)
- Whether you intend to work unsocial hours
- Whether you intend to provide overnight care
- The resources and learning experiences you have to offer the children.

Setting fees can be a difficult decision for childminders to make as, although you should be making a reasonable wage, you must also be careful not to price yourself out of the market. It is probably true to say that some parents may be prepared to pay a premium for a childminder with years of experience and relevant qualifications, however it is also worth remembering that, in the vast majority of cases, the parents own earning potential will have a huge impact on the amount of money they can afford to spend on childcare. It is important therefore that you carry out some research and get an idea of the fees other childminders in your area are charging.

Exercise

Contact several childminders in your area and enquire about their fees. Look on your local Children's Information Service website for a list of childminders in your area. This list also gives details of the service the childminders provide, any vacancies they have and how much they charge. It may also be useful to contact several nurseries in your area and enquire about their rates, in order to get an idea of what parents expect to pay.

As you are self-employed you are not entitled to the minimum wage and must not therefore base your hourly fees on the national minimum rate. However, if you employ an assistant you will be expected to pay them the minimum wage or above and we will look at this in more detail in Chapter 8.

Before deciding how much you are going to charge it is important that you look at the expenses you will incur while running your business. You will need to decide what you are intending to include in the basic fee and make a list of your charges for extras. Your basic fee should include:

- The use of toys and resources such as paint, paper, crayons, etc.
- Toilet rolls
- Drinks
- A proportion of the running costs you will incur such as heat and light and insurance (we will look at this in more detail in Chapter 8).

You may wish to charge extra for:

- Meals and snacks (although these are often included in the basic fee)
- Outings
- Petrol, if you are providing transport to schools, clubs, etc.
- Nappies, if the parents prefer you to provide them
- Formula milk, if the parents prefer you to provide it
- Special dietary foods.

You should decide on a set fee for your service and then negotiate with the parents with regard to any extras.

Nannies

There are no fixed rules concerning the level of pay a nanny should expect to receive, however, they must be paid the national minimum wage. Your age, experience, duties and location will all have an impact on the salary paid. Local nanny agencies may be able to give you some indication about the salaries paid to nannies in your area.

Methods of payment

Before signing a contract it is important to decide how you would like to be paid. Although you should be flexible to some degree, with regard to being paid it is advisable to request payment in advance.

You should consider whether you prefer to be paid:

- Daily
- Weekly
- Fortnightly
- Monthly

Remember, if you request to be paid monthly, in advance, this may be difficult for parents on a low income or who are being paid on a weekly basis themselves and you should take this into account.

You should decide whether you would like to be paid:

- In cash
- By cheque
- Directly into your bank account.

Depending on the amount of money involved, payment in cash may be difficult for some parents. Being paid by cheque can have problems for the childminder if they work long hours and find it difficult to get to the bank to cash the cheques. If you and your customers have access to Internet banking one of the easiest ways of being paid is directly into your account. This method of payment eliminates the need for you personally to go to the bank to pay in cheques or cash.

Childcare vouchers

More and more parents are being offered childcare vouchers by their employers as a work incentive. Childcare vouchers can take the form of either paper vouchers or electronic vouchers.

Paper Vouchers

These are given to the childminder by the parents, who in turn receive them from their employers as part of their salary. The parent and childminder both sign the voucher and they are then either paid into the childminder's bank account like a cheque, activated by a telephone call to the voucher provider or posted to the voucher provider to be redeemed directly into the childcarer's bank account.

Electronic Vouchers

These are by far the easiest method of voucher payment. Electronic vouchers or virtual vouchers eliminate the need for actual paper vouchers to change hands (reducing the chance of parents forgetting to bring them or them being lost in the post). Electronic vouchers are paid directly into the childcarer's account on an agreed set day.

Further information

Any childcare practitioner who is registered or approved and has a bank account in the United Kingdom can accept childcare vouchers. Before accepting vouchers you must register with the relevant voucher company by providing them with your contact details, bank account details and registration number.

Childcare vouchers were introduced in April 2005 by the government, who changed the tax rules relating to employer-supported childcare. These changes make it possible for both parents and employers to save money if the employer agrees to contribute towards their employee's childcare costs.

Nannies

Jane Davidson, the Minister for Education and Lifelong Learning, announced a proposed scheme to be available for the 2007–8 tax year, for parents in Wales who employ a nanny to look after their children, to be able to access childcare vouchers.

If a company offers its employees childcare vouchers and pays them through a pay-as-you-earn basis, then the parent can choose to have some of their salary paid in vouchers rather than in cash. By accepting these vouchers, the parent does not have to pay income tax on the first £50 worth of vouchers they receive each week. The employee and the employer also both stand to save the National Insurance contributions on this amount. If both parents are able to receive vouchers through their employment they stand to save twice as much money, making it a viable option.

Although there are no financial benefits to childminders who agree to accept the vouchers, they should in theory ensure that childcare providers are paid on time; although if you are used to being paid in cash on a set day each week this will no longer be the case as the vouchers will be paid directly into your account, probably on the same day as your original cash payment; and could therefore take several days to clear the banking systems. Also, if you accept paper vouchers you will need to take into account the time taken for posting the voucher to the company before it is processed.

Some childminders may feel that accepting payment by vouchers is not for them, however you must bear in mind that you may lose business if you refuse to accept the vouchers as they can offer parents a substantial saving in tax each month. Accepting payment by childcare vouchers definitely adds another selling point to your service and may attract more customers.

Some employers operate their own childcare voucher scheme but the majority use one of the following companies:

Accor Services **www.childcarevouchers.co.uk**
Allsave Ltd **www.allsaveuk.com**
Busy Bees **www.busybees.com**
Care-4 **www.care-4.co.uk**
Childcare Options **www.vouchers4kids.com**
Corporate Childcare Solutions Group **www.ccsguk.com**
Early Years Vouchers Ltd **www.childcare-vouchers.net**
Fair Care **www.faircare.co.uk**
Family Matters **www.familymatters.co.uk**
Imagine Cooperative Childcare Vouchers **www.childcarevouchers.coop**
Kidsunlimited **www.virtualvouchers.com**
Leapfrog **www.leapfrogdaynurseries.co.uk**
Sodexho Pass **www.sodexhopass.co.uk**

You can also obtain further information about using childcare vouchers by contacting the Daycare Trust on www.daycaretrust.org.uk or HM Revenue and Customs on www.hmrc.gov.uk/childcare.

Retainer fees and deposits

When negotiating a contract you must decide whether you are intending to charge retainer fees and/or deposits.

Retainer fee

If you have a place available and agree to reserve this place for a child in the future, it is acceptable to charge a retainer fee. The amount of the retainer fee payable should be negotiated with the parent but it is usually 50 per cent of the full fee and is paid to recompense the childminder for loss of earnings while they are waiting for the place to be occupied. You should decide how long you are willing to hold a place open for and inform the parent of the date you expect the full placement to commence. A retainer fee is not a credit towards future childcare costs but should be repaid if the place is not available on the agreed date. If a parent changes their mind and does not take up the placement then the retainer fee already paid is kept by the childminder. Although, by requesting a retainer fee you will effectively be earning money for doing nothing, you will not be allowed to fill this place with another child even for a short time. The place being retained must be available for the child whose parent is paying the retainer fee, at all times. The purpose of a retainer fee serves to provide the childminder with some income, albeit a reduced one, while waiting for the placement to commence, and serves to reassure the parent that a place will be available when required.

Retainer fees can be particularly useful for:

- Families moving to the area who have found suitable childcare but will not be needing it for several weeks.
- A mother who is on maternity leave but would like her child to have a place with a particular childminder when she returns to work. (Retainers should not be charged until *after* the baby is born.)
- The children of school teachers who may not require your service through the holidays could secure their place by paying a reduced fee to retain their place when the new school term begins.

Deposit

A deposit is a one-off fee paid by the parent to secure a place when it becomes available. Deposits are usually paid to 'book' a place already being used but which is due to become vacant shortly, perhaps because the present child's family are moving out of the area or the child is leaving to attend school. Deposits are particularly useful to secure a place that is currently serving the notice period, as a date for commencement of the new contract will be known. Deposits are usually deducted from the first week or month's fees after the placement has begun. If a child fails to take up the place then the deposit is retained by the childminder. Likewise, if a place is not available on the agreed date the deposit should be refunded.

Charging for holidays and illness

Childminders often find it difficult to decide what, if anything, to charge for holidays and illness. As you are self-employed it is up to you to decide the terms of your contract, however, you must make sure the demands on your customers are not excessive or unreasonable. Some childminders charge the full rate for their own holidays and for time taken off for illness, whereas others charge a percentage of the usual fee, often 50 per cent. It is worth bearing in mind that if you take time off work for holidays or illness then the parent may have to pay another individual to cover their childcare arrangements. If you demand full payment and they also have to pay for alternative childcare this could prove problematic. Try to see things from everyone's perspective and, while we all need a holiday from time to time to recharge our batteries, and cannot help succumbing to illness, it is also necessary to think your requests through carefully. Some childminders are unhappy charging a fee if their service is unavailable due to holidays or illness and agree to waive the fee in these circumstances. This can have the added benefit of reassuring parents that you are not likely to have lots of unnecessary days off sick as you will not get paid. The childminder can then reasonably request that the parent pays the fee in full if their child does not attend the setting for similar reasons.

Exercise

Do your homework and enquire about what charges other childminders in your area make for illness, holidays, retainers, etc. so you will have some idea of what you can reasonably charge.

Case Study 7

Julie cares for Amanda who is the daughter of two school teachers, Geoff and Susan. When the contracts were signed, Geoff and Susan agreed to pay Julie half of the usual fee in the school holidays as a retainer for Amanda's place as they would not need childcare during this time. However, at the start of the summer holiday when Julie presented the bill Susan was reluctant to pay the retainer, and said she did not see why she should pay Julie for doing nothing. Julie was upset at Susan's reaction and showed her a copy of the contract which clearly stated that a retainer was payable. Julie now feels that she should waive any future retainers but feels that the drop in income during the school holidays may prove too much for her business to withstand.

1 Do you think Julie handled this situation well?
2 What else could Julie have done in this kind of situation?
3 How might the situation have been avoided completely?

Playgroups and nurseries

If a child in your care attends playgroup or nursery and you are still considered to be responsible for them during the time they are attending these sessions, then you should be charging the full fee. Always remember that if a child arrives at your setting at 8am to be taken to playgroup or nursery for 9am and then collected again at 11.30am they will only be away from your setting for 2½ hours, not taking into account travelling time, and it will be very difficult for you to fill a vacancy for this length of time. If you are still considered to be 'on call' for the child during this period, for example if they were to become unwell and needed collecting, you will not be able to fill this place even if you were lucky enough to receive an enquiry. The parent should be charged for the full place. However, if a parent takes and collects the child themselves from playgroup or nursery and you do not actually take responsibility for them until say 11.45am then you may like to negotiate a reduced fee for this. Bear in mind though that half days are not always easy to fill and you could end up with five vacant morning places with little chance of filling them.

> As a general rule, it is probably acceptable to charge full fee for a place which is available regardless of whether it is being used or not.

Discounts

In some circumstances it may be appropriate to allow a discount in fees. However, you should think carefully about the implications this may have for your business and ensure that, by accepting a reduced fee, you will not be compromising your service in any way. Discounts are sometimes offered when two or more children from the same family attend your setting. As childcare fees can generally be quite high you may feel unwilling to charge one family for three full-time places at your usual rate. However, you must bear in mind that, although the fee you receive may be less than if you were caring for children from different families, your overheads will still be the same. You will still be expected to feed the children and provide them with toys and resources, and the running costs for your business will not be reduced. If you do decide to allow a reduction for siblings, always make it perfectly clear to the parents that the reduction is agreed when *all* the children are in attendance and if one of the children leaves, perhaps to go on to school, the fees will be revised.

Signing the contract

Before anyone signs the contract it is important to ensure that all parties involved understand exactly what is expected of them. Contracts can be purchased from organizations such as the National Childminding Association or you can devise your own. If you choose the latter option, make sure that the contract you draw up is clear and concise and leaves no room for misunderstanding or misinterpretation. Go through the contract with the parents and explain every point therein. Encourage the parents to ask questions and add to the contract to clarify any points they raise, if necessary. When everyone is happy with the content of the contract then all parties should sign and date it and copies should be retained by both the parents and the childminder. Signed contracts are legally binding documents.

The contract should include the following information:

1 The name, address and details of the child to be cared for.
2 The name, address and details of the child's parents or carers.
3 The core days and hours that childcare will be required.
4 The fee agreed and what this includes, i.e. meals, snacks, etc.
5 Details of any fees charged for:
   – Childminder illness
   – Childminder holidays
   – Child/parent illness
   – Child/parent holiday
   – Bank holidays.
6 The name of the person responsible for payment of the fees.
7 The day the payment is due and whether the fees are payable in arrears or advance.
8 Details of who is responsible for playgroup/nursery fees if applicable.
9 The items which parents are expected to provide, such as nappies.
10 Details of any fees charged for late collections.
11 The arrangements for any expenses incurred through trips and outings.
12 A review date for the contract.
13 Notice periods for holidays or termination of the contract.
14 Signatures of all the parties involved.

Reviewing the contract

You should decide how often you would like to review your contracts and record this on the contract itself so that all parties are aware of it. A review date is not a date when the contract ends; it is simply a time when all parties concerned can look at the agreement and decide whether or not it is working for them and whether any changes need to be made. Most childminders review their contracts every 6 to 12 months and find this is a good time to introduce any necessary increase in fees.

Terminating the contract

There may come a time when you or the parent needs to terminate the contract. Notice of the termination of the contract by either party should be given in writing and should not include a holiday period. In normal circumstances both the childminder and the parent should serve the full notice period as stated on the contract – usually four weeks – however if termination is immediate then payment in lieu of notice must be made.

Summary

At the end of this chapter you should be able to:

- Analyse the fees charged in your area and decide how much to set your own fees at.
- Decide which method of payment suits you best.
- Decide whether to charge deposits and retainer fees.
- Decide whether to charge for holidays and illness.
- Negotiate a contract.

Further Reading

You can get more information about childminding by requesting a copy of 'Childminding is it for you?' from Ofsted.

Ofsted helpline – 0845 601 4771.

Useful Websites

www.childminding.org
  The Scottish Childminding Association (SCMA)

www.csiw.wales.gov.uk
  Care Standards Inspectorate for Wales (CSIW)

www.ncma.org.uk
  The National Childminding Association (NCMA)

www.nicma.org
  The Northern Ireland Childminding Association (NICMA)

www.ofsted.gov.uk/about/childcare
  Ofsted website

Voucher Payment Providers

Accor Services **www.childcarevouchers.co.uk**

Allsave Ltd **www.allsaveuk.com**

Busy Bees **www.busybees.com**

Care-4 **www.care-4.co.uk**

Childcare Options **www.vouchers4kids.com**

Corporate Childcare Solutions Group **www.ccsguk.com**

Early Years Vouchers Ltd **www.childcare-vouchers.net**

Fair Care **www.faircare.co.uk**

Family Matters **www.familymatters.co.uk**

Imagine Cooperative Childcare Vouchers **www.childcarevouchers.coop**

Kidsunlimited **www.virtualvouchers.com**

Leapfrog **www.leapfrogdaynurseries.co.uk**

Sodexho Pass **www.sodexhopass.co.uk**

You can also obtain further information about using childcare vouchers by contacting the Daycare Trust on **www.daycaretrust.org.uk** or HM Revenue and Customs on **www.hmrc.gov.uk/childcare.**

Managing a Successful Business   8

National Standards
- Standard 12 – Working in Partnership with Parents and Carers
- Standard 14 – Documentation

Units of the Diploma in Home-based Childcare
- Unit 1 – Introduction to Childcare Practice (Home-based)
- Unit 3 – The Childcare Practitioner in the Home-based Setting
- Unit 4 – Working in Partnership with Parents in the Home-based Setting

Income and expenditure

As a childminder you will be classed as a self-employed person and, as such, you will be liable for keeping records of your business accounts and paying any tax and National Insurance contributions that are due.

There is no right or wrong way of keeping accounts and you are free to choose the method which suits you best, *providing* this method is accurate and up-to-date.

You may choose to record your accounts on a computer or in a book. There should be a minimum of two main headings for your accounts detailing *Income* and *Expenditure*. You may like to have a separate page for each. It is good practice to enter your account details every week and log your receipts accordingly, before filing them away to avoid losing important receipts or forgetting what has been spent. Below is an example of a simple accounts page which can be adapted to suit your own business expenses. It is possible for childminders to purchase pre-printed accounts books from the National Childminding Association (NCMA).

Remember

If you employ an assistant to help you run your childminding business you will be expected to pay them at least the national minimum wage and you will be responsible for paying their tax and National Insurance contributions.

The figures in both of the columns in Figure 8.1 should be added up and you will be left with a weekly total for income and expenditure.

Receipts are not usually required for any items under £10, however if you have a receipt it is always best to keep it. A good way of matching the receipts to the expenditure logged in your accounts is to number each receipt and write the same number next to the entry it relates to in the expenditure column.

INCOME			EXPENDITURE		
Week commencing 7 August 20xx			Week commencing 7 August 20xx		
Date	Description	Amount	Date	Description	Amount
07.08	Fees for: Sam David Isobel Catherine	 £50.00 £50.00 £25.00 £25.00	07.08	Petrol	£20.00
08.08	Fees for: Isobel	 £25.00	08.08	Toiletries Play-Doh Paint	£4.50 £4.99 £6.98
09.08	Milk refund for August	£13.66	09.08	Entrance fees to play gym Paper	£4.50 £3.99
Total		£188.66	Total		£44.96

Figure 8.1 Income and expenditure chart

As a childminder you will be able to deduct a certain amount of money from your income as 'allowable expenses'. The following list gives some of the more popular consumable items but, as with most lists, this is not exhaustive and you should bear in mind that most things, if purchased solely for the use of your childminding business, will probably be classed as an allowable expense.

Toiletries/sundries

- Toilet rolls
- Baby wipes
- Soap
- Washing-up liquid
- Tissues
- Cotton wool
- Kitchen roll
- Protective gloves and aprons
- Changing mats
- Nappies
- Nappy sacks
- Air freshener
- Disinfectant
- Cleaning products, including toilet cleaner, anti-bacterial sprays, window cleaner
- Dishcloths and floor cloths
- Bibs
- Towels
- Mops
- Hand cream
- Carpet cleaner.

Equipment

- Cots and bedding
- Pushchairs and bedding
- High chairs and restraints
- Walking reins and wrist straps
- Car seats
- Potties
- Toilet seats
- Safety equipment, including safety gates, cupboard locks, fire guards, smoke detectors, glass film, fire blankets and fire extinguishers.

Toys, games and activities

- Books, tapes, videos
- Toys, puzzles and games

- Outdoor toys and equipment
- Arts and craft materials, including paint, glue, paper, Play-Doh, crayons, felt-tip pens, pencils
- Cooking equipment and ingredients.

Training expenses

- Additional course fees which you have paid to fund further professional development
- First-aid course (to be renewed every three years).

Insurances and membership fees

- Household insurance
- Public liability insurance
- Car insurance
- National Childminding Association membership fee
- Group membership.

Remember

Childminders must take out public liability insurance as a requirement of their registration. It will insure you against legal liability arising from:

- Accidental injury or death to any person, including minded children in your care, caused by your actions or negligence.
- Damage caused to other people's property by the minded children in your care.

Nannies

If you employ an assistant you will also be expected to take out employer's liability insurance. Nannies should check that their employer has public liability insurance in place to cover personal injury if they were to have an accident in their employer's home. It is also advisable for nannies to take out professional indemnity insurance to provide them with cover in case a child suffers a serious injury while in their care.

Food and drink

Childminders have differing methods for claiming for meals. Some include the cost of the meals in their hourly rate and others charge a set fee per meal or snack.

Hours worked	Heat/Light (%)	Water Rates (%)	Council Tax (%)	Wear & Tear (%)
10	8	2	2	10
15	12	4	4	10
20	17	5	5	10
25	21	6	6	10
30	25	7	7	10
35	29	9	9	10
40	33	10	10	10

Figure 8.2 Allowable expenses: percentages claimable by hours worked

Outings

- Running costs for your car
- Car-parking fees
- Fares paid on public transport
- Entrance fees
- Food purchased during trips out

Some of the items in the lists above will be bought regularly such as toiletries, food and drink, while others such as large items of equipment, pushchairs, etc. will be one-off expenses. It is important to make sure that the cost of the consumable items you purchase for your business do not get swallowed up in your household expenses, and taking the time to do your accounts regularly should avoid this.

In addition to the expenses listed, which relate directly to your childminding business, you are also entitled to other 'allowable expenses' such as heating, lighting and water. These expenses are worked out depending on the number of hours you work per week. This does not mean the total number of hours for all the *individual* children you care for, but the total number of hours you have worked concurrently.

For example, a childminder caring for three children for 2 hours per day, five days per week, is working a total of 10 hours whereas a childminder who is caring for one child for 6 hours per day, five days per week, is working a total of 30 hours.

Figure 8.2 shows the percentages you can claim as allowable expenses depending on the number of hours you work (see above).

To work out percentages it may be helpful to use the method below:

- Firstly, work out 1 per cent of the figure. Do this by dividing the whole number by 100 (everything whole consists of 100 per cent).
- Secondly, multiply this figure by the per cent value you are working out.

For example, to find 12 per cent of £200 you would:
Divide 200 by 100 (to find 1 per cent) = 2

Multiply 2 by 12 (the per cent value you are looking for) = 24
Therefore 12 per cent of £200 is £24

Exercise

Spend a little time calculating the allowable expenses you would be able to claim if you worked a 40 hour week. You will need to look at your past fuel, water and council tax bills to work out your own deductions.

The Inland Revenue has agreed to relax the very strict record-keeping requirements which are imposed on other self-employed people so that all childminders need only submit a three-line statement of accounts to the Inland Revenue if their turnover is less than £15,000 per annum. It will still be necessary to keep a complete record of accounts in case the Inland Revenue needs to make any enquiries. If you earn less than £15,000 per annum you will need to inform the Inland Revenue of your:

- Total income for the year
- Total expenditure for the year
- Your net profit for the year (the net profit is calculated by subtracting your expenses from your profit).

Financial help for childminders

Childminders in both England and Wales may be eligible for a start-up grant to help with the costs of setting up their business. These grants are distributed by the childcare departments of local authorities and can be used to purchase toys and equipment, insurance, membership for the National Childminding Association, or registration and inspection fees. The average sum awarded to childminders in England is £300 rising to £600 in disadvantaged areas.

Figure 8.3 will help you to work out your weekly income. Figure 8.4 will help you to work out your weekly expenditure.

Total weekly income   Total weekly expenditure
£221.40   –   £212.20   =   £9.20
This is the total weekly balance.
In this instance the amount is in credit.

Childminders in Wales are entitled to the National Childminding Association's bilingual Quality Start membership and 'tools of the trade' package, together with up to £300 to be used for minor alterations to their home, as a result of Welsh Development Agency

Name	Fee/Hour		Hours		Days		Total
Sam	£2.70	x	10	x	5	=	£135.00
David	£2.70	x	8	x	4	=	£86.40
					Total weekly income	=	**£221.40**

Figure 8.3 Weekly income calculation

Food and drink	£40.00
Disposables	£13.50
Your salary + National Insurance + Tax	£150.00
Other	£8.70
Total weekly costs	**£212.20**

Figure 8.4 Weekly expenditure calculation

funding. Childminders also have the benefit of receiving a contribution towards further training costs and access to one year's business support from the NCMA.

In the past local authorities have been able to offer childminders in areas of disadvantage a 'bridging grant' if they have had a vacancy for more than two weeks. Recently this scheme has been widened and now, rather than simply having money for specific cases, local authorities can use the funding in other ways providing it 'increases the sustainability of childminders by addressing their vacancies'. It now means that local authorities can distribute the funding in a variety of ways, such as:

- Producing leaflets to promote childminding
- Providing bridging grants where necessary
- Providing training for the promotion of childminding businesses
- Funding a support worker to give advice on filling vacancies.

Childminders can claim for the cost of one-third of a pint (189ml) of milk per day for each child in their care under the age of five years. To register, apply for a form from the Welfare Food Reimbursement Unit (WFRU), PO Box 31044, London, SW1V 2FD or telephone them on 020 7887 1212. You will be provided with a form to complete and return every four months. In February 2005 the Department of Health began piloting a new scheme entitled Healthy Start in Devon and Cornwall, which allows childcarers in these areas to claim for *either* milk or a piece of fruit. If successful, the pilot scheme will be introduced across England and Wales.

Using a car for your business

If you use your car while carrying out your childminding work, you have two options with regard to claiming expenses. You can either claim:

1 **Capital allowances** – These are given on the *reducing balance* basis at an annual rate of 25 per cent (up to a maximum of £3,000 per annum) and start with the vehicle's market value. As you will probably be using your car for purposes other than childminding you will only be allowed to claim the business proportion of the capital allowance, together with all other actual running costs, such as petrol. If you choose to claim capital allowances on your vehicle you will need to keep full business accounts and will not be eligible for the concession allowing childminders to submit only a three-line statement for tax purposes to the Inland Revenue.

2 **Mileage allowance** – The approved mileage allowance payment (AMAP) is set annually by the government and states the exact figure that can be claimed for car mileage. These rates can be checked by visiting www.inlandrevenue.gov.uk.

Nannies

Nannies may have the opportunity of using their employer's car while carrying out their duties, and if this is the case, they should check that they are included on the car insurance policy. If nannies use their own vehicle they will be required to pay car insurance to cover business use, which is more expensive. If this is the case it may be worth negotiating with your employer to see whether the difference in the extra premiums can be met by them.

Using public transport

If you do not use a car for your business and choose instead to travel on public transport you can claim the costs of tickets as long as the reason for your travel is directly attributable to your childminding business. Taking children to the park or museum using the bus, for example, can be claimed. If the cost of your tickets amount to more than £10 you must obtain a receipt.

Tax and National Insurance

Although it is essential as a self-employed person to keep accounts for tax purposes, you may find that, as a childminder, you will not earn enough from childminding alone to be liable to pay Income Tax. This is largely because the expenses involved in doing the job properly can be quite high. These expenses can be offset against your gross income and will therefore reduce your net income.

Whether or not you will need to pay Income Tax will depend on whether the income you have earned is greater than your personal annual tax allowance, after you have deducted your expenses. The personal allowance for anyone under the age of 65 for the year 2005/06 was £4,895 and you would not be expected to pay tax if your earnings, minus expenditure, came to less than this figure. However, if your income is greater than your personal allowance then you will need to complete a self-assessment tax return. You may receive a self-assessment tax return even if your income is less than your personal allowance and, if this is the case, you must complete and return it to avoid paying penalties.

You can request a self-assessment tax return by telephoning the Inland Revenue on 0845 900 0404 or by contacting your local tax office. It is also possible to complete tax returns online by visiting www.inlandrevenue.gov.uk.

The amount of tax, if any, you are required to pay will be assessed on your total income minus your expenses. For example, a childminder earning £10,500 total income for the year 2005/06 is left with £4,500 after deducting all her expenses. Her personal allowance for the year is £4,895 and she has no savings or other means of income. She is not, therefore, liable to pay tax.

If you have other taxable income such as savings, a pension or another job then you should contact your local tax office for advice. It is important that you contact your tax office and notify them that you are working as a childminder, even if you have not exceeded your personal allowance and are not liable to pay tax.

Childminders with an annual turnover of more than £15,000 will be required to keep full business accounts and it may be necessary for them to seek the advice of an accountant.

VAT

In very rare circumstances childminders who are running larger businesses may cross the VAT threshold. This was £60,000 for the year 2005/06. If you consider that your business may cross this threshold you must contact the VAT national advice service on 0845 010 9000 as you may be required to register for VAT purposes. You can find out more information about VAT by visiting the website www.hmce.gov.uk.

Nannies

Nannies, unlike childminders, are employed rather than self-employed and as such it is their employers who are responsible for paying their tax and National Insurance contributions. Nannies may negotiate their wage on either a gross figure or a net figure. If the wage is based on a gross figure then deductions will come out of this amount. If the wage is based on a net amount then the employer will be responsible for paying the necessary deductions for tax and National Insurance contributions on top of this figure. It is advisable for nannies to negotiate a wage based on a gross figure, in order for them to take advantage of any government increases in the personal tax allowance or cuts in income tax rates.

National Insurance contributions

As a self-employed person you will be liable to pay self-employed National Insurance contributions unless you claim exemption because of low earnings. You should consider carefully whether or not to make contributions, as opting out may deprive you of certain benefits such as maternity and sickness benefits or a retirement pension. The National Childminding Association strongly recommends that all childminders pay Class 2 National Insurance contributions regardless of whether or not they are exempt, as choosing to pay something will protect future benefit entitlements.

Profit and loss

A successful business should be making a profit. It is important, however, to remember that a new business will not be successful overnight and will require hard work and dedication. You will need to build up custom and continue to work hard to keep your places full. It is probably true to say that most childminding businesses fail to make a profit in the first 12 months, sometimes longer, as there are numerous start-up costs involved. Childminders will be expected to pay for toys and equipment and ensure that their home is safe before registration is granted, and will therefore probably be recouping these costs for some time once customers start calling. You may also be waiting several months, after your registration has been granted, for your business to get off the ground and this can be a worrying time for childminders who need to recoup some of their setting-up costs. The trick is to buy only the basics necessary for starting your business and build on your resources as and when finances allow. Try to purchase good quality toys and equipment which will stand the test of time as cheaper versions can often prove a false economy if they have to be replaced regularly.

Your childminding business will always be in one of the following situations:

- Making a profit
- Making a loss
- Breaking even.

Obviously the most desirable situation to be in is to be making a profit. This will enable you to earn a decent wage, as well as have the extra money to re-invest in your business to purchase new toys and equipment. If your business is making a loss you will need to look closely at the way you are running things and find areas that you can cut back on until business picks up. Breaking even is not too bad a position to be in, providing you are earning a decent wage for the hours you are working and are able to provide the children with the necessary resources.

Promoting your business

If your business is making a loss you will need to look carefully at ways of turning it around. Never bury your head in the sand and hope for miracles. You may love being with children and be unconcerned whether you are making a decent living out of your work but this is not the right attitude to have. Childminders are not running a charity and you will be doing yourself a gross injustice if you are willing to work for little or no reward. You need to look at your childminding as a business and run it professionally in order to provide the best possible care for the children. You may be able to withstand making a loss for a few months, for example, if a child leaves your care and you have a vacancy, but it is essential that you look at ways of filling the vacancy before it becomes a financial burden.

If your business is making a loss you may like to consider the following strategies:

- Increase your fees – Always speak to the parents of the children you are caring for and explain to them why you feel it is necessary to increase your fees. Give plenty of notice before you increase the fees and be reasonable with the amount you are requesting.
- Increase the number of hours you are working if you are not currently working full-time.
- Advertise any vacancies you may have.
- If all your places are full, consider employing an assistant or working with another childminder to increase the number of places you have available. You must contact your regulatory body and inform them of any changes you wish to make and to request a change in numbers.
- Try to cut back on your expenses. It is important that you do not compromise the care you are providing for the children, although you may be able to cut back in some areas such as the amount of new toys you are buying.

Complaints

There may be occasions when a working relationship with a parent becomes difficult and this may be for a variety of reasons. The most common cause of conflict when childminding is a breakdown in communication; it is vital therefore that you take the time to talk to the parents of the children in your care on a daily basis. This way you can ensure that any problems are dealt with as they arise and are not left to fester.

Always deal with any complaints or disagreements in a professional manner and keep calm. Speak to the complainant politely and objectively and aim to find a compromise. Remain on a professional level at all times.

Always bear in mind that children can quickly pick up on any tension between their parents and carer and may become distressed. It is therefore paramount that any conflict is dealt with quickly, but without acting on impulse. Finding suitable solutions will often require compromise from both sides and you should be prepared to make these compromises and be flexible. In very rare cases, when a solution cannot be found, it may be best to terminate your contract with the parents as continuing to care for a child in these circumstances may be detrimental to the child in the long run.

Case Study 8

Jeremy has been caring for Poppy for seven months. As the weather has turned colder Jeremy has requested that Lynda, Poppy's mother, bring a warm coat for the daily trip to school that Jeremy has to make with Poppy to collect his own son. Lynda has forgotten Poppy's coat on several occasions making it difficult for Jeremy to take Poppy out in the cold. When Jeremy brought this oversight to Lynda's attention she snapped at him and said it wasn't such a big deal and that she couldn't remember everything. Jeremy remained calm but explained to Lynda that he had to take Poppy to school with him and that by forgetting her coat it meant that Poppy's journey was uncomfortable. Lynda said he should be caring for Poppy not collecting his own child from school. Lynda has been very frosty towards Jeremy since this exchange of words and drops off and collects her child with as little conversation between herself and Jeremy as possible.

1 In your opinion, was Jeremy right to request that Lynda bring a coat for Poppy?
2 How should Jeremy handle the current situation?

Summary

At the end of this chapter you should be able to:

- Maintain accurate records of income and expenditure for your business.
- Be aware of any financial help available for childminders.
- Understand the implications of using a car for your business and know what claims can be made against your tax.
- Understand the procedures for paying tax and National Insurance contributions.
- Analyse whether your business is making a profit or loss.
- Deal with any areas of conflict.

Useful Websites

www.childminding.org
The Scottish Childminding Association (SCMA)

www.csiw.wales.gov.uk
Care Standards Inspectorate for Wales (CSIW)

www.inlandrevenue.gov.uk
Inland Revenue website

www.ncma.org.uk

The National Childminding Association (NCMA)

www.nicma.org

The Northern Ireland Childminding Association (NICMA)

You can get more information about nannies by contacting:

www.nanniesatwork.co.uk

Nannies at Work Limited

www.nannyjob.co.uk

Nanny Job

9 Documentation

National Standards
- Standard 2 – Organization
- Standard 6 – Safety
- Standard 7 – Health
- Standard 11 – Behaviour
- Standard 12 – Working in Partnership with Parents and Carers
- Standard 13 – Child Protection
- Standard 14 – Documentation

Units of the Diploma in Home-based Childcare
- Unit 1 – Introduction to Childcare Practice (Home-based)
- Unit 3 – The Childcare Practitioner in the Home-based Setting
- Unit 4 – Working in Partnership with Parents in the Home-based Setting
- Unit 5 – Planning to Meet the Children's Individual Learning Needs in the Home-based Setting

Writing policies

A policy is an explanation of the way you deal with a particular issue. It should state the actions you will take in a particular situation. It is very important, when running a business from home, that everyone is aware of your rules and it is therefore essential that you have several policies in place to protect both yourself and your premises. What may be acceptable in one person's home may be totally unacceptable in another, and although it is important to remember that we are all different and that there are no right and wrong ways of bringing up children, you also have the right to request respect for both yourself and your belongings. A child may be allowed to use the family sofa as a trampoline at home but, if this is not acceptable to you, you must ensure that everyone is aware of it. Remember, you may not just have one child abusing your furniture every day, you may have six all bouncing up and down on your three-piece suite!

Start as you mean to go on. If you never allow a child to start behaving in a way which is unacceptable to you it will be easier for you to implement your policies. Always remember that children will, and do, push the boundaries at some point, particularly if their parents are present. Even the most well-behaved child may play you off against their parent when they have come to collect them. This is all part of growing up and a child is learning by trying to see exactly how much they can get away with! Always be consistent and stick to your rules regardless of who is present. Children need boundaries and will become confused if they are allowed to do something when their parents are present that they would not normally be allowed to do throughout the course of the day. If the television set is out of bounds to the children, do not allow them to play with the remote control just because their parent has walked through the door and you do not feel comfortable reprimanding them. If your rules are fair and consistent they will be much easier for the children to understand and accept.

You may like to consider writing and implementing policies on the following:

- Behaviour
- Equal Opportunities
- Confidentiality
- Sickness
- Fees
- Child Collection
- Smoking
- Smacking
- Complaints.

It is not necessary for you to have a separate policy for every issue; you may feel that some things are unnecessary or you may like to combine several policies together.

You should make sure that parents have a copy of all of your policies and, where possible, you should display them on the walls of your setting. It may be a good idea to ask parents to sign a form, at the same time as they sign their contract, to confirm their understanding and acceptance of your policies in order to eliminate any confusion in the future.

Everyone's policies will be unique. It is not a good idea to simply copy the wording of a policy from a friend or from a book. What is acceptable to one person may not be to another. Your policy must reflect what is acceptable to *you* and *your* setting.

The example below shows how a behaviour management policy may look, but remember, you will need to word your own policy to take into account the things that matter to *you*.

The policy should include a number of things, namely:

- Your particular ground rules
- What is considered unacceptable behaviour to *you*
- How you intend to deal with appropriate and inappropriate behaviour.

Example of a Behaviour Policy

It is my belief that children benefit most when their behaviour is managed positively and consistently. In order for all the children in my care to remain happy and enjoy their time with me, I have a few ground rules which I would appreciate everyone's cooperation in implementing:

- Children will treat each other and adults with respect
- Children will not hit, kick, pinch or bite one another
- Children will show good manners towards other children and adults
- Children will not stand on the furniture
- Children will remove their shoes when they enter my setting
- Children will not be permitted to run inside my home
- Children must be seated when eating or drinking
- Children will not be allowed to play outside unsupervised.

I ensure that I give praise and encouragement when children behave in an acceptable way and I will reward this behaviour. Children who show unacceptable behaviour will be dealt with according to their age and stage of development and my methods of discipline will vary from; distraction, ignoring the behaviour, tone of voice or, if necessary, time out. I implement a no smacking policy within my setting.

Exercise

Write a behaviour policy which would be suitable for your own setting.

Keeping records

In addition to writing and maintaining policies, there are certain other records which it will be necessary for you to keep. These records are as follows:

- Child record forms
- Records relating to the childminder and their setting
- Written permissions

- Accident records
- Assessment records
- Suspected child abuse records.

It is important that you take the time to find out as much as possible about the children you care for in order for you to be able to carry out your duties to the best of your ability. The more information you have about a child, the easier it will be for you to provide the care and stimulation that they require. Much of the information you will need will be gathered in the first meeting you have with the parents and during the child's settling-in period when you are all getting to know one another.

Child record forms

You should keep a separate record form for each child in your care which should include:

- The child's full name, address and telephone number
- The child's date of birth
- The child's parents' or carers' details including work details and where they can be contacted
- Emergency contact details
- The child's doctor's details
- Details of anyone who has been given permission to collect the child
- Details of anyone who cannot collect the child, for example, in the case of divorced parents if there is a court order against one of the parents forbidding them to have any contact with the child
- Details of any allergies or health problems
- Details of any likes or dislikes
- Information about which immunizations the child has had.

Records relating to the childminder and their setting

In addition to records for each child, you should also keep certain records available about yourself and your setting to show to parents, should they request them. These records should include:

- Your registration certificate
- Your public liability insurance certificate
- Your first-aid certificate
- Your Criminal Records Bureau Disclosure
- Your attendance register
- Your accident book
- Your emergency procedure
- The contracts you have with the parents of the children
- Details of any assistants you may employ.

Written permissions

It is very important that you have signed written permission from the child's parents for the following situations:

- Seeking medical attention
- Taking photographs or videos of the children
- Recording the children's voices
- Taking the children on outings
- Transporting the children in a car
- Carrying out observations and assessments of the child
- Applying sun protection cream to the child
- Administering medication.

Case Study 9

Georgina has just begun to care for Natalie two days per week. Natalie is 18 months old. Georgina has requested written permission from Natalie's parents to transport their daughter in her car when she takes the older children to school. Natalie's parents have refused this request, stating that they would prefer Georgina to walk the children to school rather than go in the car as the fresh air is good for the children and they are worried about the volume of traffic outside the school which they consider to be dangerous. It will take Georgina 15 minutes to walk to school with the children and on one of the days when Natalie is present Georgina will also have a nine-month-old baby with her. Georgina does not own a double pushchair but has decided to invest in one in order to carry out the wishes of Natalie's parents.

1 Do you think Georgina is right to alter her usual plans to accommodate Natalie's parent's wishes?
2 What could Georgina have done to avoid this problem arising?
3 What alternatives are there for Georgina?

Accident records

You must keep a record of all accidents that occur involving a child while on your premises. The parents should be notified of any accidents involving their child and asked to sign your record as proof that they have been informed of any injury. A child who arrives at your setting with an injury should have this explained by the parent and you should record the parent's explanation in your accident record and again request the parent to sign to acknowledge the injury.

Assessment records

If you carry out assessments of the children in your care you should share your findings with the child's parents. It is important that you work together with the child's parents in order for any assessments you carry out to be beneficial. There is more information about assessing children in Chapter 13 of this book.

Suspected child abuse records

You may have reason to suspect that a child in your care is being abused. If this is the case you must follow the actions set out in your Area Child Protection Committee (ACPC) Procedure and record everything you have witnessed. We will look at child abuse in more detail in Chapter 12 of this book.

As with all records, it is paramount that the information you keep is accurate and up-to-date. Ask parents to look over the records you keep on their children periodically, at least once a year, in order that they can update the information. Mobile telephone numbers, in particular, tend to be changed often and there is little point in you keeping records if, when you need them, you find that the information you hold is out of date.

When new children start in your setting you will collect important information from the parents about the child's history, however, it is vital that you continue to maintain a good relationship with the child's parents after the initial friendship has been established. In order for you to carry out your duties to the best of your ability and to provide the best possible care for the child, it is paramount that you value the relationship you have with the child's parents. Once the child has settled into your setting, it is this relationship which you have built up that will ensure the continuity of care which is so important for the child.

As an early years professional, it should be your ultimate goal to provide continuity between the child's home and your setting, and you must recognize the importance of sharing information about the child with their parents.

Keeping diaries

Nothing should take the place of direct conversations with the parents of the children you care for and you should make the time to speak to each other regularly, whether this is an informal chat at the end of the day or an hour's in-depth conversation over a cup of coffee. In order for you to carry out your duties to the best of your ability it is important that you liaise with the parents and share information with each other. Quite often parents, and indeed childminders, are tired at the end of a busy day and it is sometimes a relief when the last child leaves and you can finally put your feet up and relax. However, being busy or tired should not deter you from exchanging important information with the parents. Diaries can be a valuable tool for childminders but should be used in conjunction with verbal exchange and not as an alternative.

> **Nannies**
>
> Children thrive when there is continuity of care from the most important adults in their lives. A good relationship between the parents and a nanny will begin with fair terms of employment and a clear contract which defines what is expected of both parties.

A diary is a personal notebook which goes back and forth with the child between their home and your setting, and can be used by both the parents and yourself to record important information regarding the child's care. Very young babies will have a pattern for feeding and, rather than rely on memory throughout the day, it is a good idea to note down in the diary the times the baby has been fed and how much milk or food they have consumed. Similarly, sleep patterns and nappy changes can be recorded in this way. Parents can then see at glance how much their baby has been fed and how much sleep they have had that day. This kind of information can be invaluable to parents who have perhaps spent the majority of the day away from their child. If you have noticed anything unusual about a child, perhaps a baby has been difficult to settle or a child has complained of a tummy ache, note this in the diary to jog your memory but *always* discuss any problems such as these when the parent comes to collect their child in case they do not get round to reading the diary that day.

Diaries can also be very useful to note down important information such as holiday dates and price increases.

In addition to keeping a personal diary for each child in your care, you would be well advised to keep your own diary in which you can record any information which you feel may be useful at a later date. For example, if a parent is often late paying you it may be a good idea to have a record of how much is owed, the due date and the action you have taken to recoup the money due. If, at a later stage, there is any doubt or queries with regard to the money owed, you will be able to refer to your records rather than rely on your memory.

Summary

At the end of this chapter you should be able to:

- Recognize the importance of implementing policies in your setting.
- Identify which policies are relevant for your own particular setting.
- Apply methods for writing suitable policies.
- Explain why it is necessary for you to keep accurate up-to-date records.
- Identify which records you need to keep.
- Summarize the importance of keeping personal diaries.

Useful Websites

www.childminding.org
The Scottish Childminding Association (SCMA)

www.csiw.wales.gov.uk
Care Standards Inspectorate for Wales (CSIW)

www.ncma.org.uk
The National Childminding Association (NCMA)

www.nicma.org
The Northern Ireland Childminding Association (NICMA)

10 Health and Safety

National Standards
- Standard 4 – Physical Environment
- Standard 6 – Safety
- Standard 7 – Health
- Standard 8 – Food and Drink
- Standard 12 – Working in Partnership with Parents and Carers
- Standard 14 – Documentation

Units of the Diploma in Home-based Childcare
- Unit 1 – Introduction to Childcare Practice (Home-based)
- Unit 2 – Childcare and Child Development (0–16) in the Home-based Setting
- Unit 4 – Working in Partnership with Parents in the Home-based Setting

A clean and healthy environment

In Chapter 5 of this book we looked at how to make your home and garden safe for children. However, in addition to these requirements it is equally important that you ensure that your home is *clean* and that you practise high standards of personal hygiene.

On a daily basis, your home will be scrutinized by the many people you come across in your line of business, such as parents, Ofsted Inspectors, health visitors, social workers, etc. and it is imperative that your home stands up to this scrutiny. As part of the registration process you will have to demonstrate to your Ofsted Inspector that you are aware of the need for high standards of hygiene and cleanliness and that you know how to prevent the spread of infection. Adequate ventilation, together with regular, thorough cleaning routines are essential.

Some of the most common areas where germs and bacteria lurk are listed below and you must be extra vigilant to ensure the cleanliness of these areas:

1 **Changing mats and potties** – These must be cleaned every time they are used. It is possible to purchase disposable changing mats although this can prove to be an expensive option if you are caring for several children in nappies. A plastic changing mat is adequate and this should be wiped down with a disinfectant solution after every nappy change. Torn or split mats should be replaced immediately.

2 **High chairs** – These should be wiped down after every use, with a suitable disinfectant solution.

3 **Nappies and soiled clothing** – Soiled nappies should be placed in a plastic bag and disposed of in an outside bin immediately. It is possible to buy specially designed containers for disposing of nappies in which the soiled nappy is wrapped separately in an anti-bacterial film before being disposed of in a bin. However, scented nappy sacks with tie handles are an adequate and cost-effective way of disposing of soiled nappies efficiently and hygienically. Soiled clothing should be either rinsed and placed in a sealed bag for the parent to take home or washed according to the manufacturer's instructions immediately.

4 **Toilets** – These must be kept scrupulously clean at all times. Children should be taught to dispose of toilet paper carefully and to flush the toilet after every use. Think carefully about the flooring around your toilet. Ideally this will be a washable surface as it is difficult to keep carpet clean and free from germs when young children are using the toilet regularly. Special care should be taken when cleaning the toilet as the bowl (both inside and out), the seat and the handle all need regular cleaning to avoid the spread of germs.

5 **Soap** – To avoid cross contamination from bars of soap used by lots of people, it is preferable to provide liquid soap in a dispenser.

6 **Towels** – Each child should have their own towel and face cloth. If you care for a number of children it is a good idea to invest in paper towels to avoid the necessity of providing lots of separate hand towels.

7 **Pets** – Domestic animals should not be allowed near food preparation areas or where children are eating or drinking. Children should not be allowed to play near the feeding bowls belonging to pets and they should be encouraged to wash their hands after contact with animals. You should ensure that your pets are adequately treated for worms and fleas and that they have had all the necessary vaccinations.

Personal hygiene

It is important to remember that children learn through watching others and it is therefore essential that your own standards of personal hygiene are high and that children can observe you carrying out these hygiene tasks.

Washing hands is one of the most important and effective ways to prevent the spread of infection and children should be encouraged to wash their hands correctly. Hands should be washed in hot water (check the temperature is not too hot) and with soap. It should take no less than 30 seconds to wash hands correctly.

Children should be encouraged to wash their hands:

- After visiting the toilet
- After touching pets and their feeding bowls
- After coughing, sneezing or blowing noses
- After playing outside or with messy activities.

You should remember that the habits of children from different ethnic groups will differ in relation to hygiene practice and you should bear this in mind while carrying out your childcare duties. There may be strict rules about personal hygiene practices within some families, and you must ensure that you help to contribute to the children's personal hygiene in a manner which is acceptable to each individual child's family preference. For example, black skin often needs extra moisturizing and children from African Caribbean backgrounds may need their hair covering while playing in the sand to protect their hair, particularly if they have braids.

The sick child

We looked at how to write and implement policies in Chapter 9 of this book and it is probably true to say that your policy for sick children will be one of the more widely used policies and one which may be particularly open to misinterpretation. It is therefore especially important that your sick-child policy is watertight and leaves no areas open to misunderstanding. Sick children should not be in a childcare setting. In addition to the fact that they may pose a risk to others, they may also be feeling irritable or in pain and should be allowed to stay at home to recuperate. All children will get ill from time to time and it is important that you are aware of the signs and symptoms of illness and how to recognize them.

A child who is feeling unwell may respond in different ways depending on their age and the nature of the illness. Older children will be able to tell you if they are in pain or feeling unwell. There may be physical signs or a change in behaviour or a combination of the two. Babies and young children will be unable to tell you what they are feeling and it is necessary for you to be able to recognize the symptoms and act upon them accordingly.

Physical signs of illness include

- High temperature
- Shivering
- Sweating
- Vomiting
- Diarrhoea
- Swollen glands
- Pale complexion
- Deep breaths
- Racing pulse
- Rash
- Pain
- Blood in the urine.

Changes in behaviour indicating illness include

- Crying
- Being irritable
- Being quiet and withdrawn
- Being tired and listless
- Being clingy
- Loss of appetite
- Being aggressive.

The above lists are not exhaustive but they do give an indication of some of the more common signs and symptoms suffered by children who are feeling unwell. It is paramount that you know how to recognize the signs and symptoms of illness and, more importantly, that you are confident of dealing with them. All childminders must undertake pediatric first-aid training as part of their registration process and it is vital that you do not underestimate the importance of this training. A child who is unwell and contagious should be kept away from the setting. There may be times when a child becomes unwell while in your care and you will need to deal with the situation while waiting for a parent to arrive. You will need to understand the significance of any symptoms you witness and act upon them according to the age and stage of development of the child. For example, a child of 7 who has a temperature will be able to convey to you how they are feeling and they should usually be able to withstand an increase in temperature without added complications. However, a child under the age of 4 suffering from a high temperature may develop febrile convulsions. It is important that you reassure the child and make them as comfortable as possible while you wait for their parent to arrive. If a child's temperature is excessively high, (above 40°C) and you cannot control it by removing clothing and sponging with tepid water then you should seek medical advice immediately.

Case Study 10

Claire looks after Thomas who is ten months old. Thomas's dad Steven dropped him off at Claire's house at 8am this morning and told Claire that he and his partner had had a bad night as Thomas had not settled well and had woken a lot during the night. He said that Thomas may be teething and that he had put some infant paracetamol and teething gel in Thomas' bag in case Claire needed it. Claire requested that Steven complete the necessary medication forms for the paracetamol and teething gel before he left.

Later that morning Thomas became irritable. He had bright red cheeks and kept putting his fingers in his mouth and crying. When Claire picked him up he felt hot and she found it difficult to settle him. Claire immediately recognized the symptoms as teething. She removed Thomas's jumper and gave him a dose of infant paracetamol to bring down his temperature and rubbed the gel on his gums as directed on the medical form. Within half an hour Thomas's temperature had lowered and he was fast asleep. Claire continued to monitor Thomas carefully throughout the day and gave him plenty of fluids.

1 Did Claire respond to Thomas's symptoms correctly?
2 What should Claire have done if the paracetamol had not brought down Thomas's temperature?

Nannies

Nannies will usually be expected to continue to care for a child if they are sick as they will not have children from other families to consider. However, childminders must think carefully before agreeing to provide care for a child who is unwell and take into account the risk of spreading infection to the other children in their care. They also risk upsetting parents of other children if they are seen to be caring for a child who is unwell.

Administering medicines

There may be times when you will be caring for a child who requires routine medication for a chronic illness, such as asthma. In cases such as these it is important that you understand what you are administering and why. You will need to be shown how to administer the medication, for example, in the case of an asthma sufferer this would involve the use of an inhaler, and you must obtain written permission from the parent before administering any routine drugs. You should check carefully how the medication needs to be stored and keep this in a secure place out of the reach of children. It is absolutely paramount that you do not *prescribe* medication yourself. Giving a child with a raised temperature a dose of infant paracetamol may seem harmless enough, but if the child is allergic to paracetamol, or if complications arise and the child needs hospital treatment, this dose of medication can have serious effects.

If a child requires medication which is not for an ongoing illness, such as an antibiotic for an ear infection, then you must obtain written permission prior to administering the medicine and record, sign and have the log countersigned by the parent so that *all* parties involved are aware of what medication the child has been given, when it was administered and how much was administered. NEVER administer any medication without prior written permission from the parent. Always make sure you are aware what medicine you are being requested to administer to a child and why.

First aid, accidents and emergency procedures

Prevention is always better than cure. However, if you are unfortunate enough to have to deal with an accident or emergency you must remember that the way you deal with the situation will have an effect on the outcome. It is important that you remain calm and in control of the situation at all times.

If you panic and go to pieces this will have a profound effect on everyone present and have far-reaching consequences on the children present. It is in situations like these when your first-aid training will need to be put into practice and you should be aware of exactly what to do in an emergency situation. You must quickly assess the situation and minimize the risk of danger to yourself and others. Offer reassurance and ensure that you stay in control of the situation. Careful planning and prior preparation is essential in order to deal with any emergencies effectively. It is important to practise safety procedures regularly and to update contact details periodically so that you know exactly what to do and how to get in touch with a parent if the necessity arises. By thinking ahead you can be prepared for all eventualities.

Exercise

Imagine a child in your care has fallen from a swing in the garden. Write down the actions you would take to deal with the situation. Remember to consider any other children present and think about how you would assess the injury and offer reassurance to all the children. State the procedure you would follow if the child required hospital treatment.

Figure 10.1 The recovery position

In times of accidents and emergencies you will need to draw on your experience of first-aid training. However, it is vital that you know your own limitations and do not attempt to carry out any emergency procedures that you are not confident and competent to do. If the injury requires medical attention this should be sought without delay so as not to further endanger the child.

Pediatric first aid training is compulsory for all registered childminders and it is vital that you keep yourself up-to-date with this training. Most first-aid training expires after three years and you will need to enroll on another course before your existing one expires. It is also good practice to recap on what you have learnt periodically and continue to practise what you have learned in order to avoid panic at the first sign of an emergency.

Exercise

Practise putting someone in the recovery position. Did you know how to do this automatically? If not, recap on your first-aid training and if necessary enroll on a refresher course immediately.

Your first aid course will have taught you how to follow the ABC routine:

A AIRWAY   Check the child's airway for obstructions
B BREATHING   Check to make sure the child is breathing
C CIRCULATION   Check the child's circulation and ensure there is a pulse.

Finally, put the child into the recovery position as shown above.

Common minor injuries

Many minor accidents can be dealt with easily and effectively providing you have a complete first-aid box and are confident of how to deal with the situation. We will look at some of the common minor accidents next.

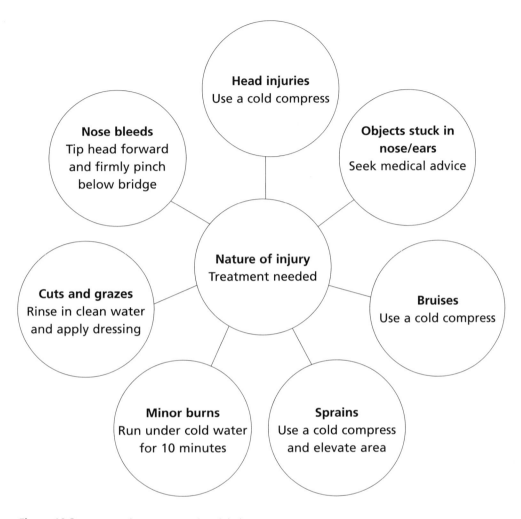

Figure 10.2 Treatment for common minor injuries

Head injuries
Place a cold object over the injury to act as a compress. Be aware of symptoms such as vomiting, drowsiness and headaches and seek medical attention if necessary.

Objects stuck in the nose or ears
Never attempt to remove the object yourself. Seek medical advice immediately.

Bruises
Use a cold compress.

Sprains
Use a cold compress and elevate the sprained area.

Minor burns

Run the burn under a cold tap for a minimum of 10 minutes; increase this to 20 minutes in the case of a chemical burn. Leave the burn uncovered.

Cuts and grazes

Rinse the area in clean water to ensure that the wound is completely clean and apply a suitable dressing if necessary.

Nose bleeds

Instruct the child to tip their head forward and gently but firmly pinch the area just below the bridge of the nose.

You must ensure that you keep a fully stocked first-aid box on your premises at all times and replenish any used items. It is recommended that you also have a small travel first-aid kit that you can take with you when on outings. You must have written permission from the parents of the children you care for before you give any first-aid treatment or medication.

You should have a fully charged mobile telephone with you when out and about with the contact details of the parents logged into it. Alternatively you should carry a small notebook or telephone book with details of contacts and loose change suitable for a public telephone in case you have to telephone parents from hospital or to inform them of any accident or injury to their child.

Remember

Prevention is always better than cure. Constant supervision of young children is essential.

Minimizing risks and preventing infection

In addition to assessing and minimizing risks with regard to toys and equipment to prevent accidents, it is also necessary for you to assess and minimize the risks in order to prevent the spread of infection. You may have a child in your care who has suddenly become unwell and started to vomit. It will be necessary for you to assess the situation and reduce the risk of infection to other children in your care while waiting for a parent to collect the unwell child. Your sick-child policy is again very important when it comes to minimizing risks and preventing the spread of infection and it is up to you to ensure that your policy states clearly what is expected of parents when their child becomes unwell and how long they will be expected to stay away from the setting.

In addition to sick children, there are many other factors which pose a threat of infection if not dealt with correctly. These factors are:

- The storage of food
- The preparation and cooking of food
- The disposal of soiled items such as nappies and baby wipes
- Correct washing of hands
- The correct disposal of medical waste, e.g. blood, vomit
- Pets.

You will need to be familiar with the correct procedure for all of the above routines and be aware of how to deal with each in a way that prevents contamination. It may be a good idea to enrol on a food hygiene course if you are in any doubt about the safe storage, handling and preparation of food. For example, are you aware of how raw foods such as uncooked meat and fish can contaminate ready-to-eat foods such as salads and sandwiches? Do you know in which part of the fridge raw meat should be stored and where to place your vegetables?

Food hygeine

- Read the labels on the packaging for guidance on storage.
- Unused food in tins should be transferred to a covered container and not left in the tins and placed in the fridge.
- Raw meat should be covered and stored in the bottom of the fridge so that it cannot drip onto other foods.
- Cooked meat and raw meat should be stored *away* from each other.
- Non-PVC film should be used to cover food as PVC can contaminate some foods.
- The use-by/best-before dates should always be adhered to.
- Avoid using foods when packaging is damaged.
- Fridges should operate below 5°C and freezers should be below -18°C.

Washing hands is probably the most important way to prevent the spread of infection. Germs are passed on easily by everything we touch. Always wash your hands:

- Before preparing foods
- Before feeding a child
- Before handling raw foods and different foods, i.e. chopping vegetables, slicing bread
- After visiting the toilet
- After tending a poorly child
- After tending to pets
- After changing nappies
- After gardening or cleaning
- After coughing, sneezing or blowing noses.

You should actively encourage the children in your care to wash their hands and make sure that you set a good example by letting the children see how often you wash your own hands and how carefully you do this. It is often difficult to explain the importance of washing hands to children as they cannot actually *see* the germs. If their hands are dirty and they wash the dirt off they may think that they are clean when in fact they may still hold many germs.

Road safety

When you are out walking with the children it is a good opportunity to teach them about road safety and point out the ways that they can keep themselves safe. You can teach older children the Highway Code and encourage them to cross the road safely. You should encourage children to:

- Stop, look and listen
- Use pelican or zebra crossings whenever possible
- Only cross the road when it is safe to do so
- Never run across the road
- Never cross the road in a place where they cannot see traffic coming in both directions, e.g. by a bend
- Never cross between parked cars.

While it is essential that you ensure the safety of the children while they are on your premises, you must be equally vigilant while out and about. As a childminder you will probably be making daily trips to support groups, playgroups and nurseries, in addition to providing a school-collection service, and it is at these times that you must plan your routines carefully and take into account all the safety issues involved.

It is essential that you gain written parental permission if you wish to take a child out with you and you should inform parents of any planned trips well in advance.

If you choose to transport a child in your own car you must have prior written consent from the child's parents. You must also ensure that you and your vehicle meet the appropriate requirements:

- You must have fully comprehensive insurance which is valid for business purposes.
- Your car must be fitted with seat belts and you must ensure that all adults in the vehicle wear a seat belt at all times, and that the children have suitable restraints, appropriate for their age, weight and size.
- The doors of the vehicle must have child locks and these should be used.
- The children must have their own seat and must not be allowed to stand or travel on someone's lap.
- When children are getting in or out of the vehicle they must do so from the pavement side.

If you plan to use public transport then you must ensure that:

- Young children are restrained with reins or wrist straps and that older children are taught to hold your hand.
- Children are taught how to behave on the street and to be aware of the dangers of traffic.
- You plan your journey in advance and know the times and places of departure of buses and trains.
- Children are sat down when travelling on buses or trains whenever possible. If all seats are taken make sure that children are standing safely with either a rail or you to hold onto to stop them from falling.
- You have a mobile telephone and contact numbers for the parents of children in your care.

As a childminder you may spend a lot of time away from the house with the children in your care. You may attend support groups, visit children's activity centres, go on day trips to parks, museums, etc. and it is very important that you understand the need to plan your journey and to take into account all the factors which may affect your trip. If you decide to take the younger children out for the day while the older ones are at school always make sure you are aware of how long it will take you to get to school and leave yourself adequate time to make the journey without having to rush or panic. You must take into account traffic delays and always allow yourself sufficient time to get to the school before the end of lessons. Remember it is better that you are sat waiting in the car for 15 minutes than for the children to be loitering on the pavement waiting for you because you have been held up in traffic, or misjudged the length of time needed for your journey. This is both a very dangerous situation and a completely unacceptable one. Children should be met at the correct time and at the agreed place and you should always make sure that you are there on time. In the very rare cases when a delay is unavoidable you must telephone the school and inform them that you have been delayed and arrange for the child to remain in school until you get there. Children can be easily upset and unnerved if the person they are expecting to collect them is late or fails to turn up and you must avoid causing this kind of anxiety at all costs.

It is important that you work towards finding a balance that allows the children in your care to remain safe while allowing them to learn and develop their independence. This is not always an easy task to perform and will depend heavily on the age and stage of development each individual child is at. The adults around them are the people who children will inevitably learn from and it is paramount that you are a positive role-model at all times.

Exercise

Devise a plan to share with the children in your care which clearly states what is expected of them when they are being collected from school. Include where the agreed pick up points are to be and what action they would need to take in the event that you were unavoidably delayed.

Summary

At the end of this chapter you should be able to:

- Explain the importance of providing a clean and healthy environment.
- Identify suitable emergency procedures for your own setting.
- Identify the signs and symptoms of a sick child.
- Summarize the procedure for administering medication to a child.
- Analyse and apply methods of minimizing risks and preventing infection.
- Explain the need for good hygiene practice.

Useful Websites

www.redcross.org.uk
British Red Cross (BRCS)

www.rospa.co.uk
Royal Society for the Prevention of Accidents (RoSPA)

www.sja.org.uk
St John's Ambulance

Equal Opportunities

11

National Standards
- Standard 3 – Care, Learning and Play
- Standard 5 – Equipment
- Standard 9 – Equal Opportunities
- Standard 10 – Special Needs
- Standard 12 – Working in Partnership with Parents and Carers

Units of the Diploma in Home-based Childcare
- Unit 1 – Introduction to Childcare Practice (Home-based)
- Unit 2 – Childcare and Child Development (0–16) in the Home-based Setting
- Unit 4 – Working in Partnership with Parents in the Home-based Setting
- Unit 5 – Planning to Meet the Children's Individual Learning Needs in the Home-based Setting

Children's rights

There are certain acts of parliament that exist and are in place to promote the equality of opportunity and the prevention of discrimination. The acts include the *Children Act*

1989 which requires that the regulatory body has a set of policies in practice for equality of opportunity and that these policies are reviewed regularly. All childcare practitioners should receive regular updates relating to equal opportunities and they should be provided with details of any relevant training as and when necessary.

The *Children's Act 1989* acknowledges the importance of the child's wishes and opinions. The act emphasizes the need for parents and carers to be *responsible* for their children rather than for them to have *rights over* them.

The United Nations Conventions on the Rights of the Child applies to everyone under the age of 18 years and consists of 54 agreed articles. Those which relate directly to childcare and education are as follows:

- Children have the right to be with their family or with the people who can provide the best care for them
- Children have the right to expect an adequate standard of living
- Children have the right to adequate food and water
- Children have the right to play
- Children have the right to be kept safe and protected from all kinds of abuse
- Children have the right to education
- Children have the right to privacy
- Children have the right to expect protection from discrimination.

It is because children cannot always stand up for themselves and be heard that this set of rights has been set up and takes into account their vulnerability.

Anti-discriminatory practice

For us to avoid discriminating against anyone, it is important that we fully understand exactly what discrimination is and what causes it. *Discrimination is the denial of equality.* This denial may come about for a number of reasons such as skin colour, religion or personal characteristics.

The main types of discrimination in child care and education are as follows:

Sex discrimination

This is when stereotypical attitudes are forced onto children, which suggest that one sex is superior to the other. Examples of sex discrimination may be when girls are offered activities which are considered feminine such as cooking and sewing, and boys are expected to take part in rough sports such as rugby.

Racial discrimination

This is when the opinion is forced on others that some races are superior to others, e.g. perhaps because of skin colour, religion or cultural beliefs.

Disability discrimination

This is when a child with a disability or impairment may be denied the opportunity to take part in activities which a more able-bodied child is offered.

> ### Exercise
>
> Think of an example which you may come across as a childminder whereby a child is discriminated against in each of the above categories. Consider ways in which you can prevent this kind of discrimination from happening in your own setting.

As a childminder you will be expected to prove your awareness of equal opportunities and anti-discriminatory practice to satisfy your regulatory body prior to registration. Adults have a responsibility to introduce different cultures to children and to encourage them to understand, value and respect the differences in others.

Discrimination can be either direct or indirect. Direct discrimination is when a child is deliberately treated unfairly, either by being denied opportunities, bullied, ignored or abused. Indirect discrimination occurs when children are made to feel uncomfortable or compromised, perhaps because of cultural differences. Indirect discrimination may be either intentional or unintentional. The effects of discrimination can vary immensely from the very obvious effects of poor self-esteem and lack of confidence perhaps caused by bullying or taunting, to the more subtle effects caused by general misunderstanding.

In order for us to ensure that we provide equality of opportunity we must first begin to understand what equal opportunity means. Equal opportunity means ensuring that *everyone* has an equal right to care and education regardless of their skin colour, religion, gender, ability, age or social background. Equal opportunity does *not* mean treating every child the same. It is important to remember that all children are not the same and therefore it would be inappropriate to treat them as if they were. Childminders must provide children with the opportunities to learn and explore which are suitable to their particular age and stage of development in order that they can develop and grow.

When introducing multiculturalism into a home-based childcare setting it is important that this is done to reflect diversity rather than as an act of tokenism. Tokenism is when the toys, books and equipment provided focus primarily on a single aspect rather than reflecting diversity. It is not appropriate to simply provide a black doll, for example, as this would mean that diversity hasn't been encompassed and would simply serve to emphasize the differences rather than show them in a positive light. Tokenism in this respect could be avoided by providing a selection of dolls showing a variety of differences such as varying skin colours, hair colours, boy dolls, girl dolls, twins, etc. Avoid using a particular culture or race as a 'theme' as, once again, this only serves to emphasize the difference and gives the impression that different cultures should be tolerated rather than understood and embraced.

Caring for children with disabilities or learning difficulties

Disabilities come in a huge variety of forms. A child may have been born with a disability or may have acquired it through an illness or accident. The disability may be very mild or it may be severe. Caring for a child with a disability can vary greatly in degree depending on the nature of the disability. What is important for a childminder to remember though is that the child is first and foremost an individual, with hopes, feelings and aspirations and the right to enjoy life in the same way as any other child, regardless of whether they have a disability or not. A child should never be defined by their disability and, as such, disabilities should not be allowed to be seen as the main part of a child's identity.

In some circumstances, it may be necessary for you to undertake specialist training if you have agreed to provide care for a child with additional needs, though in a lot of cases parents can often provide the information and guidance needed in caring for their child. If you agree to take on a child with a long-term medical condition it is vital that you equip yourself with the relevant knowledge required to provide the appropriate care for the child. Again, parents are usually the most knowledgeable people with regard to their children and may well be the greatest experts with regard to a particular disability. They will know what may trigger a certain condition, how their child reacts to the medication and what to do in the event of an emergency. Charities and support groups may also provide valuable information and support and it is advisable to work with the parents to find a solution that works well for everyone concerned.

In the past, disabled people have been treated as outcasts and because of this have suffered greatly. It is no longer acceptable for someone with a disability to have a poor quality of life and it must be recognized that they have the same goals and needs in life as everyone else. As a childminder it is up to you to ensure that the resources you provide reflect disability in a positive light and you should aim to provide images and resources which show disabled people achieving in the same way as able-bodied people. You should encourage children to look past a person's disability to see a true picture of the person themselves.

Exercise

Impairments come in a variety of forms. Make a list of some of the common impairments a child may be likely to suffer and suggest ways in which you could include them when planning and preparing activities in your childminding setting.

Children should be encouraged to ask questions in a polite and respectful manner and these questions should be answered truthfully depending on the age and stage of development of their understanding. Never encourage a child to keep quiet or ignore someone showing signs of a disability as this may lead to prejudice resulting in a lack of knowledge. However, never assume that a child who has a disability will be happy to discuss their impairment as some may have difficulty coming to terms with it and become angry or upset. It is a good idea to discuss special needs with children regardless of whether you actually provide care for a child who has them as this will encourage children to explore their own feelings and to learn about diversity.

If you agree to care for a child with a disability you may need to adapt your environment or resources accordingly. Talk to the parents of the child to get an idea of the equipment which the child relies on at home and source specialist firms where necessary.

Some of the aspects of your environment you may need to consider adapting are:

1 **Toilet** – You may need to provide a rail for support or adapt the toilet seat.
2 **Sink** – You may need to provide a step to reach the sink and adapt your taps as it may be difficult for a child to grip and turn. Levers may be more suitable.
3 **Your actual environment** – A child in a wheelchair will require much more space to manoeuvre and you may need to look closely at the layout of your furniture. Doors will need to be wide enough to accommodate wheelchair access and ramps will be necessary in place of stairs.
4 **Toys** – Increase your provision of tactile and noisy toys for children with visual impairments or provide colourful toys with flashing lights and vibrations for children experiencing hearing difficulties.
5 **Books** – Tactile books and Braille are useful for visually impaired people.

Gender

It is often assumed that boys enjoy rough-and-tumble games more than girls, and that sewing and cooking are activities more suited to girls. These assumptions are incorrect and childminders must not advocate this kind of stereotypical behaviour. A stereotype is something which is based on an assumption of what is considered to be 'normal' for a particular person. It should not be assumed that football is a boy's game and that all boys prefer to play football, than say tennis, as this is simply not the case. Cooking is often seen as a predominantly female activity, however many boys enjoy this pastime and are equally as happy as girls when baking a cake. Stereotypes can be very detrimental to a child's development and should be avoided at all costs.

Although it is true to say that a child's parents have the ultimate say in how they wish to bring their child up, they should be discouraged whenever possible from thinking that playing with dolls and dressing up is for girls and that playing with soldiers and cars should be left to the boys. It is often the case that a boy who has no sisters and is surrounded by the traditional 'boys' toys at home will invariably head for the dressing-up clothes, dolls house or pram when they arrive at their childminder's house. This is simply because these toys are new to him and he has the opportunity of exploring a whole new world of toys and resources. Children should be encouraged to take part in all the activities on offer and play with all the toys and resources available regardless of their gender.

Racial origins

Racism is the belief that one person is better than another primarily on the basis of their race. Racism has been the cause of death and destruction the world over and is something that must be challenged. It is important to remember that racism is not simply a problem of 'white' people who may be prejudiced against people with 'coloured' skin but may also be aimed at different cultures. For example, racism could be directed towards Irish or Jewish people. Children need to learn about different races and cultures and should be encouraged to accept and value these differences.

In recent times race-relation legislation, multicultural education and anti-racist campaigns have lead to a wider understanding of the problems posed by racism, however, many old prejudices still remain and these must be challenged.

Case Study 11

Anthony is a childminder caring for two children: Ben aged 3 and Jade aged 4. At the park one day Jade notices a man walking by with a turban on his head. Jade laughs at the man, points and shouts to Ben to look at the man with the big bandage on his head. Ben also starts to laugh and the man walks quickly by with his head lowered. Anthony tells Jade to stop laughing and explains that it is rude to point at people in the street and laugh. Jade and Ben continue playing and Anthony says no more about the situation.

1 In your opinion, did Anthony handle this situation well?
2 Do you think that Jade understood what Anthony had said to her?
3 What else should Anthony have said to Jade?
4 What can Anthony do to prevent this kind of situation from happening again?

As a childminder it is important that you are prepared to challenge racism and that you have the confidence to do so.

Religion

Like racism, religion has been the subject of many deaths over the years and much of this is caused by a lack of understanding. It is important that childminders seek the advice of parents with regard to any religion they may practise and that they follow these instructions. Not all members of a certain religion or culture may follow the same practices and in some cases people may adhere to the requirements more strictly than others. Religion may affect a lot of the day-to-day aspects of a child's upbringing, including diet, dress code, festivals and behaviour, and it is essential that you are aware of any aspects which may affect the care you provide for the child. Never assume that all families keep to orthodox practices as some may adopt a more relaxed approach to their faith. Childminders have a duty to promote respect, tolerance, awareness and acceptance of religious differences, and you must be sensitive to the needs of all of the children in your care.

Summary

At the end of this chapter you should be able to:

- Explain the rights of children.
- Recognize the types of discrimination.
- Identify ways of providing care for a child with a disability or learning difficulty.
- Explain how you can adapt your environment and resources to take into account caring for a child with a disability or learning difficulty.
- Identify the different ways in which prejudice can affect children.

Useful Websites

www.bda.org.uk
British Deaf Association

www.cre.gov.uk
Commission for Racial Equality

www.disabilityalliance.org
Disability Alliance

www.dlf.org.uk
Disabled Living Foundation

www.downs-syndrome.org.uk
Down's Syndrome Association

www.drc-gb.org.uk
Disability Rights Commission

www.rnib.org.uk
Royal National Institute of the Blind (RNIB)

Child Protection

National Standards
- Standard 12 – Working in Partnership with Parents and Carers
- Standard 13 – Child Protection
- Standard 14 – Documentation

Units of the Diploma in Home-based Childcare
- Unit 1 – Introduction to Childcare Practice (Home-based)
- Unit 3 – The Childcare Practitioner in the Home-based Setting

What is child abuse?

Child abuse is behaviour that causes significant harm to a child. There are four types of child abuse and these are defined below:

- **Emotional Abuse** – This is when a child is deprived of love and affection. They may be repeatedly rejected or humiliated.
- **Sexual Abuse** – This is when a child is directly or indirectly exploited or corrupted by involving them in inappropriate sexual activities. Showing children pornographic material is also classed as sexual abuse.
- **Physical Abuse** – This is when a child is hurt physically, including hitting, kicking or inflicting pain. Poisoning, drowning or smothering are also forms of physical abuse.
- **Neglect** – This is when a child is denied the appropriate care, including love, attention, safety, nourishment, warmth, education and medical attention.

Abuse can have long lasting traumatic effects which can damage a child's development emotionally, physically and psychologically. A child who has been abused may grow up with feelings of inadequacy and have difficulty forming happy relationships. Some may even become abusers themselves.

Children have the need and right to be in an environment where they feel happy, safe and secure and it is your duty, as a childminder, to ensure that these needs are met and, should you suspect that a child in your care is being abused, you must act upon your suspicions. It is not an option to ignore or turn a blind eye to your suspicions hoping that someone else will deal with the problem. You have a duty and responsibility to put the child's needs and welfare first.

In order to try to understand abuse and why it occurs, you must first be aware that it can occur in any family structure. Abuse does not discriminate and it is important that you do not assume that it can only happen to children from poor families or single-parent families. Even children from 'respectable' backgrounds can be subjected to abuse.

In most cases children who suffer from abuse do so at the hands of someone who is known to them. Although it has been suggested that a high proportion of abusers have themselves been abused and therefore know of no other way of dealing with children, this is not always the case. Abuse is often the result of a combination of social, economic, medical, environmental and psychological factors and it is important to remember that children of any age can be vulnerable to abuse.

Types of abuse

We will now look at the four types of abuse in more detail.

Emotional abuse

A child who is constantly deprived of love and affection will quickly lose confidence and become nervous and withdrawn. Being subjected to continual threatening behaviour in the form of verbal abuse or shouting can have lasting effects on a child. It is very difficult to see any signs of emotional abuse as the effects are rarely physical. Children who are subjected to emotional abuse are often vulnerable and have a low opinion of themselves. They constantly crave attention and will often put their trust into anyone who shows them any sign of affection.

Figure 12.1 Some signs of emotional abuse

Sexual abuse

A child who is used by an adult for their own sexual gratification is said to be sexually abused. It is very important to remember that not all sexual abusers are male. Children may be subjected to sexual abuse through bribery, threats or physical force and sexual abuse can take the form of fondling, masturbation, sexual intercourse, oral sex, exhibitionism or through the showing of pornographic materials. A child who is being sexually abused may show both physical and emotional signs.

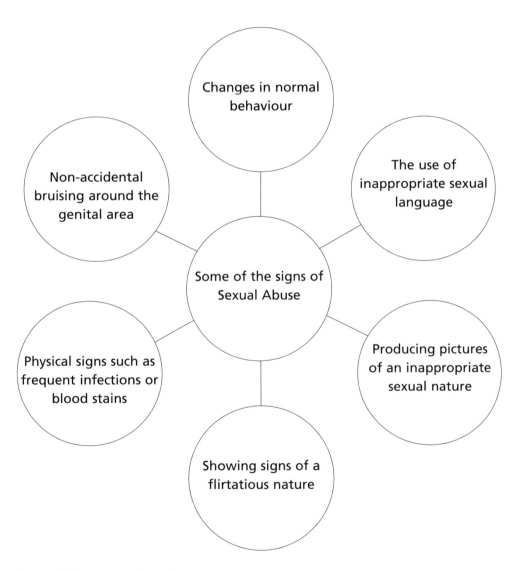

Figure 12.2 Some signs of sexual abuse

Physical abuse

A child exposed to physical abuse is suffering from the deliberate infliction of pain and injury. Physical abuse may take many forms and includes hitting, shaking, biting, burning, cutting, squeezing and poisoning.

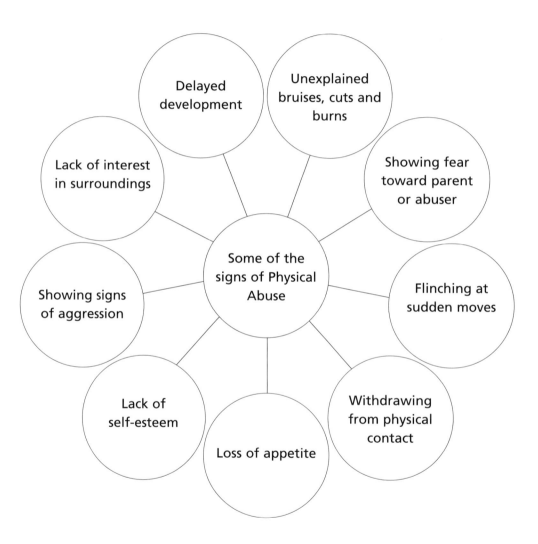

Figure 12.3 Some signs of physical abuse

Neglect

A parent who persistently fails to provide the basic physical needs for their child is guilty of neglect. Neglect can take many forms including failing to provide adequate food or clothing, failure to seek medical advice when necessary or leaving the child unattended.

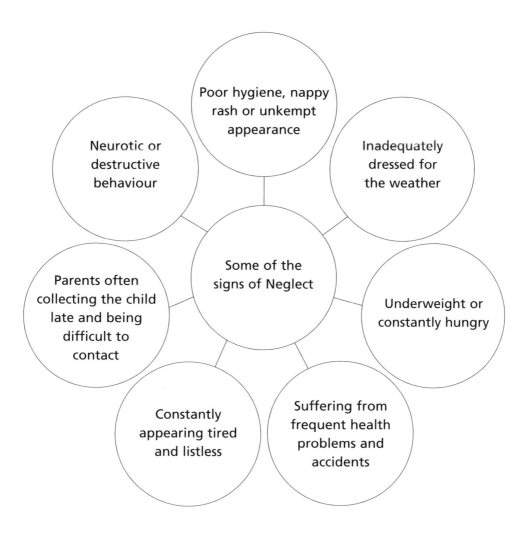

Figure 12.3 Some signs of neglect

Recognizing the signs and symptoms of abuse

The above gives some indication of the signs and symptoms suffered by children who are being abused. It is important to remember that no two children are the same and no two circumstances will mirror one another. It is for this reason that you must remember that these are the most *common* signs of abuse and a child may suffer from one or more of the symptoms. As a childminder or nanny you will be in the best possible situation to monitor a child's behaviour and will inevitably notice any changes almost immediately. Unlike children who attend nursery schools and may be cared for by several different carers, you will have built up a trusting relationship with the child and should notice any worrying signs, symptoms or changes in their usual behaviour.

The chart below shows the *common* sites for both accidental and non-accidental injuries.

Common sites for *accidental* injuries

- Forehead
- Chin
- Nose
- Knees
- Elbows
- Forearms
- Spine
- Hips
- Shins

Common sites for *non-accidental* injuries

- Lips and mouth
- Eyes
- Ears
- Cheeks
- Skull
- Chest
- Stomach
- Buttocks
- Back
- Backs of legs
- Upper or inner arms
- Genital or rectal areas
- Soles of the feet

Although the above lists give the most common sites for injuries, you must bear in mind that not all injuries on the shins, for example, may be accidental. Persistent or experienced abusers will often try to hide the injuries they inflict on the child or make them *appear* accidental. It is just as important to recognize the *type* of injury, as well as the *site* of the injury when trying to decide whether any abuse has taken place.

Bruising

When the result of an accident, bruises are usually scattered and irregular. Bruises which are the same colour suggest they occurred at around the same time. It is important not to confuse birthmarks or Mongolian blue spots with bruises. When bruising is non-accidental it may appear in the shape of an implement which has been used to inflict the injury such as a belt or buckle. The bruises will be regular and of varying colours indicating both old and new bruises. Bruising on the lips, eyes, ears and mouth are usually associated with non-accidental injuries.

Burns and scalds

The parent of a child who has suffered from an accidental burn or scald should furnish you with details of the injury and offer a logical explanation. Medical attention should have been sought in severe circumstances and the wound should be dressed appropriately. When a burn or scald is not accidental if may appear in difficult-to-reach places such as the buttocks or back and therefore would not suggest self-infliction. The burn may take on the appearance of the object which was used to inflict the injury such as a cigarette.

Fractures and breaks

Broken bones in young children are most common on the arms and legs and, occasionally the ribs. Children under the age of two years rarely experience accidental fractures. Broken bones or fractures in varying stages of healing should be viewed as suspicious.

Genital injuries

Many young children suffer from constipation or threadworms and discomfort around the anus may be suffered as a result of this. Nappy rash in babies may also provide soreness and blistering. However you should treat any bruising, bleeding or infection of the genital areas with suspicion.

Cuts and grazes

Accidental cuts and grazes are usually minor and require no treatment. Deep incisions or large untreated scratches should be viewed with suspicion.

Bites

A child may sometimes be bitten by another child in the course of everyday play. However, bite marks which are too large to be inflicted by another child or those which show an adult-teeth pattern should give cause for concern.

There are many factors which may be associated with child abuse and it is important that you do not make any assumptions as to the kind of people who are likely to inflict abuse on their children. As we have mentioned before, there is no set pattern for abuse and it can occur in any family structure. As a childminder or nanny you must be vigilant when assessing the evidence you have and avoid stereotyping gender as this may result in signs of abuse being ignored. For example, a boy who shows a lack of emotion and appears dirty and unkempt may be seen by some as a typical boy who prefers to be independent and enjoys getting dirty. However, it may also mean that signs of neglect are going unrecognized. Would the same assumptions apply if it was a girl who was dirty, unkempt and lacking in emotion?

Disclosures of abuse

In addition to you actually noticing possible signs or symptoms of child abuse which give you cause for concern, it may be that a child themselves provides you with a disclosure of abuse. There are two ways in which a child may disclose the possibility that they are being abused:

- **Overt Disclosure** – This is when a child actually approaches you and tells you verbally what is happening to them.
- **Covert Disclosure** – This is when a child uses pictures, play or body language to draw your attention to what may be happening to them. Covert disclosures are less obvious and should be interpreted carefully keeping things in proportion without ignoring the evidence.

If you suspect a child is being abused it is essential that you act upon your suspicions. Listen to what the child tells you without interrupting, asking questions or prompting them. Stay calm and talk to the child in a manner appropriate to their level of understanding.

If a child tells you they have been abused:

- Stay calm
- Speak to the child gently and allow them plenty of time to tell you in *their own words* what they want to stay
- Never ask leading questions or point the finger of blame
- Do not interrupt the child or put words into their mouth if they are having difficulty expressing their feelings
- Offer reassurance and tell the child they have done the right thing by confiding in you
- Never promise to keep their disclosure a secret. You will not be able to keep this promise and you could seriously harm a child who has placed their trust in you and then feels you have let them down.

Recording signs of abuse

Any child in your care who has suffered from an injury, however minor, should have this injury recorded. If a child arrives at your home with an injury, you should seek an explanation from the parent about the nature of the injury and record the details. These records would be absolutely vital in a child-abuse case. A child may be suffering from injuries or neglect over a sustained period of time and it is only by carefully logging injuries and incidents that you and other professionals may be able to recognize a pattern of abuse forming. The records you keep, while primarily for the protection of the child, should be kept with the cooperation of the parents.

When recording details of injuries or suspicions it is vital that you stick to the *facts*. Never let your own opinions or judgements hamper your reasoning, and if a child discloses an incident of abuse, record what they have said *exactly* using their own words and do not be tempted to elaborate or add to their disclosure.

Case Study 12

Joanne has been childminding Jasmin for eight months. Jasmin lives with her father Dominic and her twelve-year-old sister Juliette. Jasmin's mother died two years ago when Jasmin was just 18 months old. It has become clear to Joanne that Dominic struggles to keep up with a full-time job and caring for his daughters and often collects Jasmin late. Jasmin and Juliette appear well cared for and are clean and appropriately dressed, but Dominic always seems to be in a rush when he drops off and collects his daughter and Joanne finds it difficult to speak to him.

Last week Jasmin arrived at Joanne's house upset and it was obvious she had been crying. Dominic offered no explanation for his daughter's distress but later that morning Jasmin told Joanne that her daddy had smacked her because she would not eat her breakfast. Joanne prompted Jasmin to explain what had happened and questioned the child about the smack, how hard it had been, where she had been hit and whether she was smacked often by her daddy. After the conversation Jasmin began crying again and said she wanted to go home. Joanne was convinced that Dominic was physically abusing his daughter.

1 In your opinion what did Joanne do wrong on this occasion?
2 What reasons do you think Joanne has for assuming that Dominic is abusing his daughter?
3 Do you think these are reasonable assumptions for Joanne to make?
4 What should Joanne do now?

Procedures to follow if you suspect child abuse

All childcarers have a duty to report their suspicions relating to abuse. It is perfectly normal that you should feel apprehensive and scared. You may feel that you are betraying the child's parents or that you have jumped to conclusions. However, if you are familiar with the signs and symptoms of neglect, and you have any reasonable doubts about the safety of a child in your care, you have a duty to report your suspicions. It is the welfare of the child which must take priority at all times.

If it is appropriate, you may like to speak to the child's parents first about the change in their child's behaviour or if the child has said something to you which is giving you cause for concern. The nature of your suspicions and the relationship you have with the parent may however make speaking to them inappropriate. All childminders should be aware of the procedure which they are expected to follow should they suspect a child in their care is being abused or neglected and you should ensure that you are familiar with this procedure. You may report your concerns to the appropriate authority or, alternatively, you may like to contact the NSPCC. Both social services and the NSPCC have a duty to investigate any reports they receive. It is vital that you remain professional at all times, only report the *facts* and respect confidentiality.

After you have reported your concerns to the appropriate authority a decision will be made by them as to whether a referral should be made. This is where the information supplied by you may be crucial in building up a background of knowledge about the child. It may be that no action is taken at this stage and you may be requested to continue to monitor the situation and record any further concerns you may have. If, however, it is decided that further action needs to be taken, this will be done by social services and not by *you*. Although you should be informed that a response has been made, you will not be notified of the action taken as this will remain confidential with the child protection agencies. If action is taken it will be necessary to interview the child and contact the parents. Enquiries may be made to other professionals such as doctors, health visitors, schools, etc. to build up an accurate picture of the child's situation. In some cases a child protection conference may be arranged. However, it is not always necessary for the childminder to attend.

Exercise

Think about your own knowledge and experience with regard to child abuse. Would you be able to recognize signs of abuse and feel confident dealing with any such issues? Find out about any further training available in your area and consider enrolling on a suitable course.

Allegations against childminders

There may be times when an allegation is made against you. At times like these it is important to record everything that has been said and, if you are a member of the National Childminding Association, it is a good idea for you to contact them and seek their advice. You may experience a variety of feelings including anger, upset and distress if an allegation is made against you. However, it is important that you remain calm and deal with any allegations rationally. Listen to what the parent has to say and then calmly put your own point of view across and explain the situation in your own words. Childminders and nannies are particularly vulnerable to allegations as they usually work alone and do not have the added support of co-workers. The teenage sons of childminders are particularly vulnerable to having accusations made against them and you should consider protecting yourself and your family in the following ways:

- Behave in a professional manner at all times
- Maintain confidentiality at all times

- Report any concerns or suspicions you may have about ill-treatment or abuse to the appropriate authorities
- Keep accurate up-to-date records of any accidents or injuries to children in your care
- Ensure that you tell parents of any accidents or injuries to their child immediately
- Ensure that you notify parents immediately if you notice a change in their child's usual behaviour
- Never handle a child roughly or inflict physical punishment
- Never ask a child for a cuddle, always take your cue from them
- Never allow children to be cared for by someone who is not authorized to do so
- Always act in a responsible manner while in the company of children and use appropriate language
- Never leave the children unattended
- Encourage children to become independent as soon as possible particularly when carrying out personal tasks such as visiting the toilet
- Keep up-to-date with your own training
- Teach children how to protect themselves and stay safe.

Where to seek support

If you have had to deal with an incident of child abuse or have had an allegation made against yourself or a member of your family, you will probably be experiencing a wide range of feelings. It is vital that you seek support to deal with your own feelings and you may like to do this by contacting:

- The National Childminding Association, if you are a member
- Social workers
- Your health visitor
- Your doctor
- A child-protection office.

Summary

At the end of this chapter you should be able to:

- Describe the different types of child abuse.
- Recognize the signs and symptoms of abuse.
- Explain how to record signs of abuse.
- Identify disclosures of abuse.
- Identify ways of protecting yourself against allegations.
- Summarize where to seek support.

Useful Websites

You can find more information about child abuse by contacting the National Society for the Prevention of Cruelty to Children (NSPCC) or visiting their website **www.nspcc.org.uk**.

www.childline.co.uk
  Childline

www.kidscape.org.uk
  Kidscape

www.yesican.org
  International Child Abuse Network

Routines and Planning

National Standards

- Standard 3 – Care Learning and Play
- Standard 5 – Equipment
- Standard 6 – Safety
- Standard 8 – Food and Drink
- Standard 9 – Equal Opportunities
- Standard 12 – Working in partnership with Parents and Carers
- Standard 14 – Documentation

Units of the Diploma in Home-based Childcare

- Unit 1 – Introduction to Childcare Practice (Home-based)
- Unit 2 – Childcare and Child Development (0-16) in the Home-based Setting
- Unit 4 – Working in Partnership with Parents in the Home-based Setting
- Unit 5 – Planning to Meet the Children's Individual Learning Needs in the Home-based Setting

The importance of planning

Planning is an important part of a successful childminding business. In order for your business to run smoothly and for you to be organized and efficient, you will need to look ahead and plan your days. There is no right or wrong way to plan, but the method you choose must be easy for you to implement and must take into account the needs of the children in your care.

Apart from the obvious day-to-day planning, which takes into account what needs to be done and at what time, for example, school drop-off, playgroup, lunch, school collection, etc., it will also be necessary for you to look at ways of planning to take into account the needs of the individual children in your care. You may like to work with the parents of the children when planning activities in order that you can ascertain together the child's strengths and weaknesses and decide on which goals and achievements to aim for. It is a good idea to involve parents in the decision of appropriate activities whether this is in written form or verbally.

Some childminders find it easier to plan their activities around a theme or topic and these can be tailored to suit the likes and preferences of the children in your care. Themes and topics can be planned according to the time of the year, for example, spring, summer, autumn or winter, and the children can be encouraged to take part in activities associated with the seasons. You may like to do a display for the wall or take the children on a nature walk looking for colourful leaves in the autumn, or pretty flowers in the summer. Celebrations such as Christmas, Easter, Divali and the Chinese New Year also provide excellent themes for planning children's learning and play. Depending on the age of the children you are caring for you may also like to introduce topics such as colours, numbers, shapes and telling the time into your everyday planning. It is always important to remember that, although useful, plans should not restrict children from being allowed to play spontaneously, and time should always be allowed for free play with planned activities interspersed.

Planning for children's learning and development can be divided into three categories, namely, short, medium and long-term.

Short-term planning

This type of planning can be used for a specific activity or perhaps for a full day's or week's activities.

Medium-term planning

This type of planning usually extends over a period of 3 to 4 weeks.

Long-term planning

This type of planning can be spread over the course of a year. Long-term planning is a good way of covering all areas of growth and development for, say, a two-year-old, and it will enable you to take into account events and festivals over an extended period of time.

In order for you to work effectively you will need to grasp the basics with regard to planning. Planning your daily, weekly and monthly activities need not be difficult. We all spend some of our time planning whether we realize it or not. It may not be apparent, but when you are deciding what to make for dinner each day you are using a form of planning. You think about who you are cooking for, how many people you are going to feed, what you are going to make, what ingredients you will need, which items you will need to shop for and which you already have, the time you will need to prepare and cook the meal and when it needs to be ready for. By simply making a meal from start to finish you have effectively 'planned' your time. You will need to do this in the course of your working day. Planning is essentially about preparing, making arrangements and then checking that the arrangements you have made are actually effective.

The planning process consists of four separate steps, namely:

- Plan
- Observe and assess
- Evaluate
- Implement

It is not particularly necessary for you to write down your plans or complete charts, however, it is often useful to have some kind of written record for you to look back on in order to build up a collection of activities and topics which you can refer to in the future. It is a good idea to record which activities and topics were particularly enjoyable or useful and whether any changes need to be made before trying out that particular activity again. Before deciding how to record your planning it is necessary for you to decide which goals you wish to develop with each particular child. Talk to the child's parents and work out together which areas of the child's development you are going to concentrate on and set a time scale for achieving the agreed goals.

A childminder's plans, with the aim of helping a child to recognize colours, may look like this:

Example: Helping a child to recognize colours

Short-Term Plan

Activities might include:

- Baking a cake and decorating with red icing
- Using red Play-Doh
- Painting with red paint.

Medium-Term Plan

Extend the child's awareness of different colours by introducing another primary colour.

Long-Term Plan

Complete the aim of helping the child to recognize the four primary colours.

It is important to remember when making your plans that babies and young children are learning all the time through their senses, and recognize the way they explore their surroundings. You must ensure that you relate your own plans to the child's growth and development. Long-term plans should, for example, include the following areas of growth and development:

- Emotional
- Social
- Sensory and intellectual
- Physical
- Language and communication.

Your overall aims when planning play and activities for the children in your care should be:

- To encourage the child to reach their full learning potential
- To meet the child's individual developmental needs
- To meet the child's individual learning needs
- To build on the existing knowledge and skills of the child.

It is important to remember that, while careful planning of appropriate play and learning activities is an essential part of a childcare practitioner's duties, these plans must always be *flexible* and allow for each child's individual interests. Be careful to ensure that unplanned, spontaneous play opportunities are always welcomed. A walk in the sunshine after a rain shower to splash in puddles and look at rainbows, or playing in an unexpected snowfall can provide wonderful opportunities for a child to explore and develop their knowledge and skills.

In addition to spontaneous play and activities that you yourself have arranged for the children, you should also allow time for the children to have the freedom to choose which toys they wish to play with and which activities they wish to take part in. It is very important that young children are allowed freedom of choice to extend their own feelings, ideas and experiences.

Observing and assessing children

When you have planned your daily, weekly and monthly activities and decided upon the goals you wish to aim for, it is important for you to be able to observe and assess the children in order to ascertain whether your plans have been successful.

Observing a child means that you are watching and studying what they do. You will be observing children all the time while they are in your care to make sure they are safe, to make sure they have the appropriate toys and equipment to play with, to see whether they are tired or hungry or whether they need a nappy change. This kind or observation will come automatically to you as you are a professional person who is knowledgeable

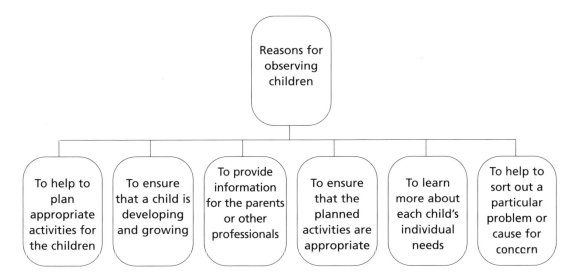

Figure 13.1 Reasons for observing children

about the care of young children and you are aware of their needs and requirements. There are, however, many more reasons why it is necessary for you to observe children, such as those in Figure 13.1.

The nature of a childminder's job means that you will be very busy throughout your working day and it is therefore necessary for you to choose a method of observing and assessing the children in your care which is easy for you to understand and, more importantly, implement. Try not to see observation and assessment as an additional task but as an essential one which will enable you to be aware of the things the children in your care can do, what they are almost capable of doing and what they need assistance with. Observing and assessing children will not only help you to pinpoint where a child is at in terms of development and growth but it will also help you to identify any problems or concerns.

There are several methods of observing children and each individual will have their own preference as to which method they prefer. It may be necessary for you to use several methods of observation during the course of your work depending on whether you require a quick, informal observation or an in-depth account. The figure below shows different ways of observing children.

Written observations

These help us to record information about a child's growth and development or their behaviour over a short period of time. Written observations require very little planning and preparation and can usually be done quickly at any time.

Figure 13.2 Methods of observation

Checklists and tick charts

These can be particularly useful to record what stage a child is at, for example, how many colours they can recognize, how many numbers they can count in sequence, whether or not they can recognize the letters of the alphabet. Checklists and tick charts are quick and simple to use and are particularly helpful at future dates to see how a child has developed and whether there are any changes since the last observation.

Participative observations

These are when you yourself actually take part in the activity with the child. The main disadvantage of this type of observation is that it can be difficult for you to write notes and record what is happening at the actual time and you may therefore have to rely heavily on your memory to record your observations at a later date.

Naturalistic observations

These are, as the word suggests, 'natural' observations of what the child is doing during the normal routine of the day. This method of observation is particularly useful to record how children respond and behave spontaneously.

Structured observations

These are when you observe a child in a situation that you have set up yourself. For example, you may like to record how a child manipulates various tools during a painting session, and by providing the child with a selection of different sized brushes, sponges, rollers, stamps, etc. you will be able to observe how the child copes with the different tools.

Event sampling

This is used to observe and record patterns of behaviour. Event sampling can be particularly useful if you or the child's parents wish to change some part of the child's behaviour, for example, tantrums. By using event sampling you will be able to record the child's behaviour at certain times of the day and ascertain whether anything in particular triggers a tantrum, when they happen, how long they last, etc.

Time sampling

This is another form of event sampling, only this time you observe what the child is doing at fixed intervals, for example, every hour throughout the whole day or every 30 minutes throughout the afternoon.

Tapes and videos

These are really only beneficial for observing children if they are not aware of their presence. You may find that a child who knows that a video camera is pointing at them will play up and act out of character making your observation unnatural and therefore ineffective. A tape-recorder may be easier to hide but the disadvantage here would be background noise if you are caring for several children. If you do choose to use tapes and videos to observe the children in your care make sure that you always get the written permission of the parents before making any form of recording of their child.

It is important, when observing children, that the information you gather is accurate, however, you must also be aware of your own limits and not attempt to make your own diagnosis of a problem or concern. While the information you have gathered and recorded may well be useful it is the responsibility of other professionals to diagnose a child.

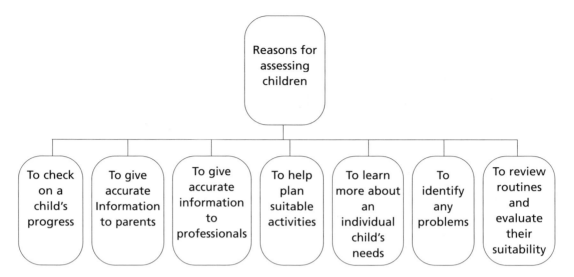

Figure 13.3 Reasons for assessing children

There is little point in carrying out observations on the children in your care if, after doing these observations, you do not assess your findings. As a childminder you will have the advantage of knowing the children in your care well and being in a position to work with them closely on a daily basis. This closeness will enable you to see how the children are growing and developing. By using your observations you will be able to assess the point each child is at and you will then be able to plan appropriate routines and activities to suit each individual child. You need to be aware of the importance for your routines to be changed as the children you are caring for grow and develop and your observations will enable you to see easily when a child is ready to be weaned, to start using a potty, to practice using scissors, etc.

Daily routines

In addition to taking into account ways of planning for children's learning experiences, it is vital that you plan to take into account the other aspects of your day. As a childminder you may spend a large amount of time out and about dropping off children and picking them up from various groups, clubs and schools. It is absolutely essential that you plan ahead and ensure that you have left sufficient time for your journey so as not to have to rush and put the safety of children at risk. Traffic volumes can never be accurately anticipated and you must ensure that you leave ample time for your journey to enable children to be at school on time and it is vital that you make sure you are there to collect them when the doors open. There is no excuse for a childminder to be late and children should never be left hanging around the playground alone waiting to be collected. If you are going to be late due to unforeseen circumstances make sure that you have made plans to ensure that the children know there is a delay and telephone the school to let them know how long you will be.

Depending on the number and ages of the children they are caring for a typical childminder's daily routine may look something like this:

TIME	ACTIVITY OR PLANNED ROUTINE
8.00am	Arrival of children – Breakfast time
8.45am	Set off on journey to school
9.00am	Drop children off at school and playgroup
9.10am	Arrive back home from school. Morning play activities.
10.00am	Snack
10.15am	Visit to library
11.30am	Playgroup collection
11.50am	Prepare lunch
12.15pm	Lunch
12.45pm	Set off on journey to nursery
1.00pm	Drop child off at nursery
1.10pm	Arrive back home from nursery. Nap time and quiet activities.
2.30pm	Play activities
3.15pm	Set off on journey to collect from nursery and school
3.30pm	Collect child from nursery
3.35pm	Collect children from school
3.50pm	Arrive back home from school and nursery
4.00pm	Tea or snack and drink
4.15pm	Afternoon activities, time for homework, etc.
5.45pm	Start to tidy toys away and visit the toilet in time to go home
5.50pm	Parents start to arrive to collect children
6.00pm	Last child leaves setting after chat with parent about their day

Each childminder's daily routine will, of course, be unique to them and you will need to adapt your own routines accordingly. You may, for example, not have a child who needs to go to playgroup or nursery but you may have a six-month-old baby whose routine will need to incorporate feeds, naps and nappy changes.

Food and drink

In addition to planning your routines and activities you will also need to look at the kind of meals and snacks you are intending to provide for the children you are caring for. It is up to you to negotiate with the child's parents which, if any, meals you are prepared to provide. Whereas some childminders provide cooked meals, others only give the children sandwiches and some even request that parents provide their own food for their children in the form of a packed lunch. How you choose to plan your mealtimes is of course up to you. However it is important to remember that some children may be spending up to 10 hours per day in your care and therefore sandwiches may not be entirely appropriate. Whatever decision you come to it is important that you work together with the child's parents to provide a healthy nutritious diet for the children. Figure 13.4 shows a week's planned menu for two children aged 3 years and one aged 4.

MEAL/ SNACK	MON	TUES	WEDS	THURS	FRI
BREAKFAST AT 8.00am	Weetabix with milk	Porridge with milk	Rice Krispies with milk	Weetabix with milk	Porridge with milk
SNACK AT 10.30am	Milkshake and fruit	Fresh fruit juice and a piece of fruit	Milkshake and a sultana and oat cookie	Fresh fruit juice and a piece of fruit	Milkshake and a slice of melon
LUNCH AT 12.15pm	Shepherds pie, vegetables and gravy, and cherry pie with custard	Cod in breadcrumbs, parsley sauce, mashed potato and vegetables, and fresh fruit salad	Roast beef and Yorkshire pudding with new potatoes and vegetables, and lemon mousse	Chicken and vegetable casserole, and chocolate fudge cake with cream	Meat and potato pie with fresh seasonal vegetables, and strawberry trifle
SNACK AT 3.00pm	Drink and a biscuit	Milkshake and fruit	Drink and a fruit scone	Milkshake and fruit	Drink and a biscuit
TEA AT 4.30pm	Sandwiches, crisps, fruit, yoghurt, cake and drink	Scrambled egg on toast, yoghurt and drink	Vegetable broth and wholemeal bread, yoghurt, fruit and drink	Sandwiches, crisps, fruit, yoghurt, biscuit and drink	Baked beans on toast, fruit, yoghurt and drink

Figure 13.4 Suggested planned menu

It is very important that you liaise with the parents of the children you are caring for in order to provide the children with a diet suitable to their needs and to ascertain whether there are any food allergies or cultural preferences that you need to be aware of.

Exercise

Plan a healthy menu for a week for three children aged 2, 3 and 4 years. One of the children has a milk allergy and you should bear this in mind when planning suitable meals.

Nannies

It is probably much easier for a childminder to plan and prepare a healthy balanced menu for the children in their care as they have sole responsibility for buying the food. **Nannies,** on the other hand, may be restricted by their employers' shopping habits as the bulk of the main shopping will probably be done by them. It is important therefore that nannies should discuss food and nutrition with the parents of the children so that they can work together to find the best course of action for providing the children with a healthy balanced diet.

Food allergies

A food allergy is an abnormal response of the immune system to what is otherwise a harmless food. Around 5 per cent of children have food allergies and most will outgrow their allergy. Sufferers of nut allergies, however, are considered to have this allergy for life. Allergies to peanuts, nuts, fish and shellfish cause the most severe allergies, although milk is the most common of food allergies in children.

Ninety per cent of all food allergy reactions are caused by just eight foods. These foods are:

- Milk
- Peanuts
- Tree nuts, including almonds, pecans and walnuts
- Eggs
- Fish
- Shellfish
- Wheat
- Soy

Symptoms of an allergic reaction can be varied but will usually include:

- Vomiting

- Diarrhoea
- Eczema
- Wheezing
- Cramps
- Difficulty in breathing

Symptoms of an allergic reaction to food may be experienced within minutes of ingesting the food; they can alternatively take up to an hour to become apparent.

Dietary differences

It is important to recognize and cater for differing dietary needs and this should not only be the case if you are caring for a child from a different culture from your own. All children should be introduced to a variety of different foods and you can do this by offering foods which are associated with certain religious festivals. For example, the Christian tradition of serving mince pies at Christmas and pancakes on Shrove Tuesday can be done alongside offering Chinese food to celebrate the start of the Chinese New Year, or poori to celebrate Diwali.

Diets vary immensely and can differ according to belief or preference. Vegetarianism, for example, may be chosen for several reasons including religious or cultural beliefs or simply concern for the welfare of animals.

Catering for Different Diets

It is essential that you check with the parents of the children you are caring for to ascertain exactly what their child is allowed to eat. When you have been told the type of diet the parents wish their child to follow you *must* respect these wishes at all times.

- *Vegetarians*
  People who do not eat meat and fish. Many people call themselves vegetarian while simply avoiding eating red meat but still eating fish and poultry.
- *Lacto-vegetarians*
  People who avoid eating meat and fish, however they still eat dairy products.
- *Lacto-ovo-vegetarians*
  People who eat the same as lacto-vegetarians but also eat eggs.
- *Vegans*
  People who eat no animal products whatsoever and stick to a diet of fruit, vegetables, cereals, nuts, seeds and pulses.

Case Study 13

Victoria is a childminder who cares for three boys all aged three years. One of the boys is a vegetarian and Victoria has discussed his dietary requirements with the child's parents. At lunchtime today Victoria served two of the children sausages with mashed potatoes and peas, while the child who is a vegetarian was served a vegetable lasagne. John, the vegetarian child, got upset when he saw that the other children were eating different food and said he wanted the same as his friends. Victoria tried to explain to John that his mother didn't like him eating sausages but this just made the situation worse and ended up with John refusing to eat anything at all.

1 In your opinion did Victoria handle this situation well?
2 What could Victoria have done differently to avoid this kind of situation in the future?
3 Should Victoria inform John's parents of the incident?

Key Cultural Differences

Hindus – Orthodox Hindus are strict vegetarians and a small minority are vegans. While some will eat dairy products and eggs others refuse eggs due to their belief that they are a potential source of life. The cow is considered to be a sacred animal to Hindus and they therefore do not eat beef. Pork is also refused as the pig is considered an unclean animal. Wheat is used to make certain types of bread such as puris and chapattis.

Sikhs – Most Sikhs will not eat beef or pork. Although some Sikhs are vegetarians, many will eat lamb, fish and chicken. Wheat and rice are staple foods in the Sikh diet and fasting is widely practised.

Muslims – Like other Asian communities Muslims do not eat beef or pork. Their staple food is wheat in the form of rice and chapattis and again fasting is practised.

Jews – Pork is forbidden to Jewish people, as is shellfish. All animals and birds must be slaughtered in accordance with the Jewish dietary laws to render them 'kosher' or acceptable. Jewish people never cook or eat milk and meat products at the same time.

Afro-Caribbean – The majority of the Afro-Caribbean community are Christian and include a wide variety of European foods in their diet. They also eat traditional foods such as coconut, green banana and yam.

Rastafarians – The majority of Rastafarians will only eat foods which are considered to be in a whole or natural state and they will not consume processed or preserved foods. Most Rastafarians are vegetarians.

There are certain things you can do to ensure that the food you prepare for the children in your care is healthy and nutritious and that mealtimes are enjoyable:

- Offer a wide selection of different foods and, if a particular food is refused at first, try offering it again at a later stage as children's tastes change often.
- Avoid adding salt or sugar to food that you are preparing.
- Never use food as a bribe, reward or punishment as this may lead to eating disorders in later life.
- Avoid giving children lots of unhealthy snacks throughout the day such as crisps, biscuits and sweets. Try to get them to stick to proper mealtimes.
- Avoid fizzy drinks wherever possible, and offer water or fresh fruit juice instead.
- Do not over fill a child's plate, and take into account each child's individual appetite when planning and serving meals.
- Set a good example yourself. If children see you eating healthy food they are more likely to follow suit than if they see you tucking into a bar of chocolate while offering them a stick of celery!

Equipment checks

Another very important routine which childminders should follow is that of checking their toys and equipment. You should regularly carry out a risk assessment on your equipment and premises. The home and garden pose many potential risks to young children and while it is impossible to eliminate all of these risks it is necessary for you to recognize them and, wherever possible, reduce them.

There are three steps which should be followed in order to carry out a risk assessment.

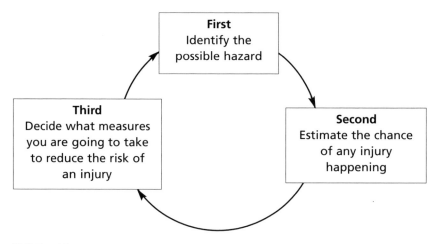

Figure 13.5 The risk assessment process

It is important to remember how quickly children grow and develop and you must bear this in mind when carrying out your risk assessment. A baby when placed on the floor, may not be in any danger from a small toy however, several weeks later this same child may be in danger of choking if they have learnt to roll over and reach out. It is vital therefore that you practice safe methods of childcare at *all* times in order to avoid complacency and to reduce the possible hazards. Young children do not understand the consequences of their actions and will rarely be able to fully understand any possible danger and it is therefore your job to do this for them. *You* are the person who must ensure that the risks are assessed and reduced and that the children in your care are free to play out of harm's way.

As part of your duties you should set aside time periodically to check your premises and equipment in order to confirm that you are providing a safe environment for the children in your care. It is a good idea to make a note in your diary, perhaps every month, to do a thorough check on all your equipment. Toys will get broken and damaged regularly and in addition to a thorough monthly check you would be well advised to check these daily when you put them away to make sure that there are no broken or missing parts.

Large items of equipment such as cots, pushchairs and high chairs should be checked to ensure that there are no missing parts or screws which need tightening up. Check restraints for signs of fraying and replace if necessary.

Outdoor equipment should also be checked regularly and a thorough examination of swings, slides, climbing frames, etc. should be made after a long period of inactivity, for example over the winter months when the cold weather may have corroded some parts or screws may have worked loose. You may find it helpful to make a note of the date and description of the equipment you have checked and any repairs you have found necessary.

In addition to checking your toys and equipment for signs of wear and tear it is very important that you check the batteries in your smoke alarms regularly. Make a note in your diary of when the checks are due and when the batteries were changed.

Exercise

Make a list of all the large items of equipment you have such as pushchairs and high chairs and make regular checks on these items, logging the date and your findings next to the appropriate item on the list.

Fire drills

It is essential that you prepare and practise a fire drill with the children in your care and they must be familiar with the routine so that in the event of an emergency all the children know what is expected of them and they can carry out the procedure with as little fuss as possible. The more familiar a child becomes with a particular routine the less likely they are to be phased in the unfortunate event of a fire on your premises.

Exercise

Write your own fire drill and emergency evacuation plan to use in your setting and begin to practise these periodically with the children.

The evacuation procedure you decide to put in place will depend entirely on your premises. You should consider your escape routes carefully and take into account the ages and abilities of the children you are caring for. You will also need to take into account the location of the fire and what you would do if your main escape route or exit is blocked. The majority of fires are started in the kitchen therefore is it really a good idea to plan an escape route through this room?

You must practise your fire drill regularly at different times and on different days to ensure that *all* the children are aware of the procedure and know what is expected of them in the event of a fire. It is pointless practising your fire drill on the first Monday of every month if you have several children who only come to you on Wednesday, Thursday and Friday. Children must understand the need to leave the building as quickly as possible, without panicking and you should explain to them that they will need to leave behind their toys, coats and other possessions.

Summary

At the end of this chapter you should be able to:

- Recognize the importance of planning your daily routines.
- Describe the different categories of planning.
- Apply planning in your daily routines.
- Explain the importance of observing and assessing children.
- Identify reasons for observing and assessing children.
- Give examples of methods of observing children.
- Evaluate your own daily routines.
- Identify ways of providing healthy meals and snacks.
- Give examples of food allergies and their symptoms.

- Describe the different cultural diets and how you can apply these in your setting.
- Assess the need for equipment checks.
- Analyse the importance of fire drills and identify a suitable evacuation procedure for your own premises.

Useful Websites

www.allergyfoundation.com
British Allergy Foundation

www.asthma.org.uk
Asthma UK

www.diabetes.org.uk
Diabetes UK

www.eczema.org.uk
National Eczema Society (NES)

www.edauk.com
Eating Disorders Association (EDA)

www.hda.nhs.uk
Health Development Agency (UK)

www.nutrition.org.uk
British Nutrition Foundation (BNF)

www.vegsoc.org.uk
Vegetarian Society

Health Information Wales Tel: 0800 665544

14 Care, Learning and Play

Chapter Outline

The information in this chapter directly relates to:
- Standard 2 – Organization
- Standard 3 – Care, Learning and Play
- Standard 5 – Equipment
- Standard 12 – Working in Partnership with Parents and Carers
- And *all* the units of the Diploma in Home-based Childcare

What is play?

It is often wrongly assumed that children are born with the knowledge of how to play. In fact children *learn* how to play from their parents and carers. There are no age, gender or ability restrictions on how to play and everyone should be allowed the chance to explore and learn from the things around them.

When asked what play is, most people would probably think of 'having fun', or 'messing around'. There are many different types of play and children should be allowed to experiment. Children play in a variety of different ways and for varying reasons.

Childminders have a responsibility to encourage the child they are caring for to develop and learn in every way possible and, in order for you to be able to do this, you need to be aware of how to adapt your routine and use the resources available to promote this development. It is not necessary for you to purchase lots of expensive toys. In fact it is probably true to say that a child's own imagination is the best 'tool' they can have and it is important that you encourage the use of a child's imagination as much as possible.

Types of play

There are three main types of play. These are solitary play, parallel play and spectator play.

Solitary play

This type of play is, as the name suggests, when a child plays alone. Most children under the age of two play in this way as they have not yet learned to play interactively. Although, as a child gets older, they usually enjoy playing with others, there is no actual age limit on solitary play and even older children often feel the need for space and sometimes do not wish to socialize. If a child does not wish to join in group activities, preferring to play alone, you should respect their wishes and ensure that your own routines allow for this.

Parallel play

The next step on from solitary play is parallel play. This is when children do not actually play *together* but simply *alongside* one another. Parallel play usually occurs in children around the age of two years. The children may be playing with the same toys but in a completely unconnected way. They may watch one another, share and communicate but without actually playing cooperatively.

Spectator play

This type of play often occurs between solitary and parallel play and is a phase that most toddlers go through. Children watch others around them without actually taking part in the game or activity. Older children may also experience spectator play particularly if they are new to a setting or situation and are still finding their feet. Spectator play is a valid form of play and can be a good learning experience. Usually children will join in, when they have watched the others and found their confidence. Although you can encourage children to join in never underestimate the importance of watching and learning and do not force a child to join in until they are ready to do so.

Appropriate play and learning activities in the home

It is all very easy to go out and buy toys and resources for children to play with, providing the money is available to do so. However, as a childminder it is important to remember that you will probably be caring for a number of children of varying ages and at differing stages of development. It will be very expensive if you are relying on bought toys and resources alone to stimulate the children in your care as you will need a wide variety of play equipment to keep everyone happy and entertained. It is important, therefore, that you look at ways of providing play activities in your home using the resources already available. Heuristic play, where you allow children to explore, discover and learn for themselves, is an essential part of learning for children.

Exercise

Think of all the everyday tasks you do as part of your usual routine and write down how many of these tasks can be adapted to include the children you are childminding. The tasks may take longer to carry out with the help of a young child but you will be helping the child's development by allowing them to take part in these activities.

Figure 14.1

Some of the everyday tasks you may like to include the children in follow.

Washing up

Children learn a lot from being allowed to play in water. In the summer months it may be possible for the children to play outdoors in water (with supervision at all times), however, in the colder months this will not be possible. By allowing the children to help you wash up you can still encourage them to bang and splash without harm or damage to your home. Encouraging this type of activity links the home setting with the childminder's setting as children will be used to playing in the bath at home or perhaps helping their parents wash up. Talk to the children while carrying out this activity to help their development. For example, you could explain where the water goes when you pull the plug, why we have drains, etc.

Washing clothes

Although the majority of us will own a washing machine and therefore the actual washing of clothes is ultimately left up to the machine to do, it is possible to include children in the sorting of the clothes once they have been washed/dried. Allowing the children to sort the socks into pairs and fold the clothes encourages mathematical development. Encouraging the children to ask questions will again help to promote the child's all round development.

Setting the table

This task is very good for helping children to sort, count and match. Encourage the children to count how many people will be present for the meal and to work out how many places need to be set. Think about the meal itself and allow the children to decide which cutlery will be needed, how many spoons, forks, etc. they need to get out.

Tidying up

All children like to make a mess! Emptying boxes seems to hold an endless fascination for young children, however, it is equally important that they learn the necessity for helping to tidy away after they have enjoyed playing. You could encourage early mathematics by helping the children to sort and match the toys into the correct boxes. Most children enjoy being helpful so make the most of this by encouraging them to help tidy up at the end of the day.

Shopping

Start by making a shopping list with the children. This will help to encourage memory skills as you can give each child one or two items from the list that they will be responsible for. Encourage the children to look for, select and pay for their 'own' items to give them the feeling of responsibility. When back at home allow the children to help you unpack the items and put them away. This will make them feel important and responsible, in addition to helping them understand the concept of size and weight. Talk to the children while they are carrying out the tasks describing how heavy or light the packages are so that they can relate to the differing weights.

Cooking and preparing food

The beginnings of science are derived from cooking and preparing food. Children should be encouraged to count, weigh and measure and cooking is an excellent way of doing these tasks. Younger children will learn how to use certain utensils and equipment while older children will grasp the concept of how food changes when heated or cooked.

Nannies

Nannies may well be expected to carry out light housework duties in addition to caring for the children, and these can be excellent opportunities to involve the children in real-life situations. You could link shop play, for example, with a trip to the supermarket.

There are many other ways you can encourage children to develop through taking part in everyday domestic activities and these may include:

- Watering plants
- Preparing and sharing snacks
- Washing hands and faces
- Dusting
- Gardening.

Using topics and themes

Introducing topics or themes using displays is a good way of exploring issues in a positive way. Obviously how and where you make your display will largely depend on the space you have available, but displaying a child's work attractively gives them a strong sense of self-worth and encourages them to feel proud of their accomplishments. If you are unhappy about using your living room walls to display the children's art work perhaps you might like to consider the use of a pin board or even buy large scrap books so that each child can have their own 'topic' book. Magnetic surfaces such as fridges and freezers can be used to display art work attractively without damage to wall surfaces, as can windows or tables. Using your own initiative and imagination will encourage children to use theirs!

Themes can be very useful, however, it is important that you do not fall into the trap of tokenism when using themes to introduce culture or religion. (Chapter 11 covers tokenism in more detail). Always make sure that your themes reflect diversity. Themes can and have been successfully used to explore topics such as:

- The seasons – spring, summer, autumn and winter
- Celebrations – Christmas, Easter, Divali, Chinese New Year, etc.
- Food
- Weather
- Sport
- Colours
- Numbers
- Animals.

Exercise

Choose two from the above categories and list how you could successfully incorporate them into a theme. Give details of how you would display your theme, i.e. on a wall, table or scrap book, and indicate the issues you will cover. Explain what you hope the children will learn from your theme and give examples of how you will encourage their development using your chosen theme.

Now list another five topics that you consider would make good themes and promote a child's development.

Child development

Before we can begin to encourage and promote a child's development and provide them with the vital learning opportunities they need we must look at the main developmental stages in a child's life.

As a child grows and develops their needs change. It is often very confusing both for parents and childcarers to understand exactly what a child should be doing and at what age and this is simply because there is no such thing as a 'typical' child. All children develop differently and at varying speeds. It is more important to focus on steady development rather than setting milestones for the children to reach at set ages. The stages listed below give an indication of the developmental stages but are not set in stone and should only be used as a guide. Remember, although some babies can crawl at seven months, others may not do this until they are well over 12 months and others may never crawl at all. Some babies are confident walkers at nine months old while others are 18 months old before they take their first steps. As you spend time caring for a particular child you will notice the things they are confident in and which areas they require help and assistance with. It is the child's *personal* stage of development which you should focus on and promote.

Birth

A new born baby needs little in the way of toys and activities and relies heavily on physical contact, reassuring voices and familiar faces.

Six weeks

A baby of around six weeks old needs things to look at and listen to in order to promote sensory development. They may be able to smile and produce gurgling noises.

Three months

Babies of around three months can 'swipe' and should be provided with suitable objects to swipe at. Colourful, noisy rattles and other toys to kick and hold are also useful.

Six months

At this age many babies will be able to sit and roll from back to front. Picture books and activity toys are particularly suitable at six months.

Nine months

At nine months a baby can usually sit up and reach for toys. They may be able to get themselves into a sitting position unaided and may also be crawling. At this age provide picture books and noisy, brightly coloured toys and activities. Simple action rhymes and songs may also be enjoyed.

Figure 14.2

Twelve months

By now the child may well be able to stand unsupported and could even be walking. You should be encouraging the use of simple words and introducing games which encourage the child to hide and find objects.

Eighteen months

At 18 months most children can walk steadily for short distances. You should by now be introducing music and dance in addition to everyday speech. Children of this age can usually throw a ball, stack bricks, match shapes, hold a crayon and enjoy push-along toys.

Two years

At two years of age a child can usually confidently walk and run and should be able to master steps (two feet to a step). They can often jump with two feet together, squat to play with toys and kick and throw a ball. Children of this age will probably enjoy a wide variety of play activities including ride-on toys, jigsaws, Play-Doh modelling, painting, threading, music, etc.

Three years

By now the child can probably walk up stairs independently using alternate feet. They may be able to peddle a tricycle, cut with scissors, paint confidently with a large brush and use a spoon and fork. Their vocabulary may be well in excess of 800 words and their coordination skills may be well established. Children of this age often enjoy imaginative play, arts and crafts, outdoor play and stories and books.

Four years

Children of this age are becoming more stable and emotionally secure. They are more confident in their play and activities and are becoming more accurate. They can usually throw a ball with aim and are more controlled when using scissors and crayons.

Five to six years

By now most children will have started school and may well be able to read, write, skip, ride a bicycle, catch a ball with one hand, hit a ball with a bat and produce imaginative artwork using a variety of colours. Favourite activities for this age group include ball games, arts and crafts, dressing up and role-play, Lego and construction toys and playground activities, such as ball games, climbing frames, bicycles, etc.

Seven to eight years

Children between the ages of seven and eight years are becoming confident and independent. As they become more aware of the world around them and strive to achieve their independence they may become frustrated and show aggression. Although the pre-occupation with dressing-up and role-play usually subsides by this age, the activities enjoyed by most children between seven and eight years of age is very much the same as between five and six, with perhaps the added introduction of more complex resources such as telescopes, magnifying glasses, microscopes and more intricate construction materials.

Exploring the five senses

All initial learning is done through the senses. Very young babies use their sense of sight, sound, smell, taste and touch to get to know their surroundings but, as children grow older, these senses become less dominant. It is important, however, that children are encouraged to experiment and you should provide different tastes, smells and textures as routine in your childminding setting.

It is important for children to learn to use their senses to the full and the most effective learning occurs when children are offered a variety of learning experiences which encourage the use of these senses.

There are many ways in which you can encourage sensory development and we shall now look at some of these.

Sight

Young babies are unable to focus very well and can only see things clearly from about 25cm from their nose. From the age of around four months a child can usually focus on objects at almost any distance. Children love brightly coloured objects and toys and you should try to provide a good selection of age appropriate toys and equipment. Eye catching, colourful wall displays are also a good way of promoting sight.

Sound

Sound is incorporated into our everyday lives in a variety of ways. It is very rare for us to be in a silent environment for very long. There is usually some kind of sound occurring at most times, whether it is voices, traffic, dogs barking, doors shutting, kettles boiling, etc. However, children can also be encouraged to make their own kinds of noise by using musical instruments and singing. Try getting the children to close their eyes while you carry out an activity and encourage the children to guess what you are doing just by listening to the sounds you are making. Try turning the pages of a magazine or newspaper, pouring a drink or bouncing a ball and see if the children can work out what you are doing by relying solely on their sense of hearing.

Touch

Although very young babies cannot hold or grasp objects, they start learning about the world around them through touch from birth. It is important that you provide a wide range of safe, tactile objects for a baby to explore. Before a baby learns to hold, usually at around three months old, they enjoy swiping at objects. Think about providing a mobile or activity bar so that the baby can enjoy reaching out and swiping. Older children can be encouraged to explore their sense of touch by providing them with a wide range of materials such as sand, water, clay, Play-Doh, finger paints, etc. Mixing and kneading pastry and dough is also an excellent way of developing the sense of touch.

Taste

We have taste buds on our tongues, in our cheeks, in our throats and on the roof of our mouths. There are four primary tastes which are important to human beings and these are:

- Bitterness
- Sweetness
- Sourness
- Saltiness.

Although our taste buds can be damaged if we eat or drink things which are very hot or cold, our bodies have the capability of repairing our sense of taste when necessary. Children's tastes change often, and a young baby who appears to dislike a food one day may happily take it a couple of days later and it is important that you continue to introduce and re-introduce foods periodically. Children should be encouraged to try a variety of different tastes and you can do this by introducing 'tasting sessions' to your childminding routines. You may have a theme for the Chinese New Year for example and this would be a good opportunity for introducing the children to Chinese food by providing small amounts of noodles, rice, prawn crackers, etc. for them to taste.

Smell

Taste and smell go together which is why when we have a cold and cannot smell, our food often lacks flavour. However, we use our sense of smell in many ways other than when eating. Encourage children to use their sense of smell by playing games with them. Blindfold a child and get them to guess what is before them simply by using their sense of smell. Do not allow them to touch or see the object. For this game to be successful you will have to choose suitable smelling objects such as a highly scented flower, a peeled orange or lemon, herbs, spices, etc.

There are many other ways of promoting a child's sensory development. Think about providing a treasure basket for a young baby (we will look at this in more detail later in this chapter) or a sensory garden for older children. This can take the form of a large planted tub or a complete area of the garden, depending on the space you have available. Think about planting things which can stimulate all the senses, such as:

- **Sight** – Brightly coloured flowers of differing shapes and sizes
- **Smell** – Scented flowers and herbs
- **Taste** – Fruit trees or bushes, salad or vegetables
- **Sound** – Grasses or reeds which blow in the wind and rustle with movement
- **Touch** – Shrubs and plants with rubbery or feathery leaves which are safe to touch. Select trees with particularly rough or smooth barks.

The seven 'Cs' and SPICE

The 'seven Cs' is a way of looking at growth and development in children. Each of the 'Cs' is linked to an area of development as stated below:

- **C**onfidence
- **C**ompetence
- **C**reativity
- **C**ooperation
- **C**oordination
- **C**oncentration
- **C**ommunication.

Another approach to looking at the various aspects of a child's development is known as SPICE. SPICE stands for:

Social development
Physical development
Intellectual development
Communication development
Emotional development.

Although a child's development is being broken down into categories when using the seven Cs or SPICE, it is vital that we realize that children develop as a whole and not in separate areas. By using these methods, however, we can monitor a child's progress and check that we are providing for every aspect of their all-round development.

We will now look at the five categories of SPICE in more detail.

Social development

There are three main aspects associated with social development and these are:

- Learning self-reliance
- Developing relationships with others
- Making decisions, taking responsibility and giving opinions.

As part of social development children will learn to share and take turns, play and work cooperatively, help others and work out how to deal with disagreements.

Exercise

Think about the children you care for and, using one of the children, give an example of how you would support their social development while they are in your care.

Physical development

There are two main kinds of physical development which we need to focus on and these are:

- Movement and gross motor skills
- Hand–eye coordination and fine motor skills.

Movement skills include crawling, walking, running, jumping, skipping, hopping, climbing and balancing. Gross motor skills include throwing, catching, kicking and bouncing.

Hand–eye coordination is the ability of a child to connect what they do with their hands with what they can see. For example, building a tower with Duplo bricks. Fine motor skills include holding, grasping, picking things up, using crayons, paint brushes and scissors, threading, etc.

Exercise

This time think of ways you can support one of the children in your care with their physical development. Give examples of activities you can provide which will promote hand–eye coordination, movement and gross and fine motor skills.

Intellectual development

Intellectual development takes many forms and will include:

- Building attention span
- Building memory
- Developing concentration
- Extending imagination and creativity
- Understanding information gained through the use of the senses
- Learning about basic concepts including numbers and counting, colours and shapes, sorting and matching, size and weight, etc.

> **Exercise**
>
> Give examples of the types of activities you could introduce to your childminding setting which will help you to promote the children's intellectual development.

Communication development

Much of every kind of learning depends heavily on the understanding and acquiring of language. Children should be encouraged to develop their vocabulary in order to ask questions, explain how they feel and what they need and to talk about their experiences. There are two kinds of language. The first is *receptive language*. This is language that is understood by the child. For example, if a child can understand the instruction 'go and get your coat' but cannot actually say the word 'coat' they would be using receptive language. The other type of language is *expressive* and this is when the child actually speaks the words themselves.

Communication is not simply the use of the spoken word and may also take the form of body-language and the tone of the voice. It is important that you realise that non-verbal language can be interpreted in different ways and, as a childminder who may be caring for children from different cultures, you must be aware of this. For example, in some cultures it is considered polite to look an adult in the eyes when they are speaking, however in others this is a sign of disrespect.

> **Exercise**
>
> Give an example of how you could support communication development in the children you are caring for.

Emotional development

The four most important areas of emotional development in children are:

- Coping with new situations
- Developing self-control
- Dealing with their own emotions
- Developing perceptions about themselves.

Everyone deals with new situations differently and, while some children cope admirably and take most things in their stride, others may take a long time to find their confidence and settle into new situations. As a childminder it is important for you to look at how you can encourage children to cope with new situations in a way that is best for them, as you may well be the person who has to help them through the transitional periods of starting playgroup, nursery and school. It is important that children are given time to adjust to any changes and that you have reasonable expectations about each child's ability to understand what is happening.

It is vital for children to develop self-control in order that they can learn to control their own behaviour and be accepted in society. As a childminder you will be able to encourage them to do this by providing clear boundaries for behaviour which are consistent and fair. Always make sure you praise behaviour that has lived up to your expectations and encourage the children in your care to explore their feelings and express them in order for them to learn self-control. Help children to remain calm, and when their emotions threaten to overwhelm them, offer reassurance.

Encourage children to develop a feeling of self-worth by giving lots of praise and encouragement for the things they have done well in and achieved rather than focusing on their mistakes. Show respect for the child's background, traditions and culture.

Exercise

How could you support the emotional development of the children in your care? Give examples of how you would encourage a child to cope with starting school for the first time. What resources could you provide to help the child cope with the change in their daily routine?

Birth to Three Matters

The Birth to Three Matters framework is designed to support children in their earliest years. The purpose of the framework is to provide those who are responsible for the care and education of babies and children from birth to three years with the support, information and guidance needed. The framework uses the child as its focus and it identifies four 'aspects' which celebrate the skill and competence of babies and young children. These four aspects are:

- A strong child
- A skilful communicator
- A competent learner
- A healthy child.

A Strong Child

In order for a child to become strong and develop into a capable and confident person they require a nurturing environment from the very outset. A baby requires a key person who will support, love and encourage them.

The components that make up a strong child are:

1 Me, myself and I
2 Being acknowledged and affirmed
3 Developing self-assurance
4 A sense of belonging.

A Skilful Communicator

Babies and young children need to mix in order to develop social relations. They need to learn the importance of friendships, emotions and language.

The components that make up a skilful communicator are:

1 Being together
2 Finding a voice
3 Listening and responding
4 Making meaning.

A Competent Learner

Even from birth, babies are able to distinguish between things and show preferences. As they use their senses to explore the world they need to be allowed to share their thoughts and feelings and identify with others.

The components that make up a competent learner are:

1 Making connections
2 Being imaginative
3 Being creative
4 Representing.

A Healthy Child

In addition to having nutritious food and being free from illness, children need to be loved and cared for and made to feel special. Their emotional well-being, together with their physical needs, all have to be addressed. Children have the right to be protected and should be kept safe and encouraged to make healthy choices.

The components that make up a healthy child are:

1 Emotional well-being
2 Growing and developing
3 Keeping safe
4 Healthy choices.

Caring for babies and toddlers

Although caring for babies and toddlers can be immensely rewarding, it is also very demanding and exhausting. Babies rely solely on their carer and, while they are with you, this responsibility is yours. If you choose to care for a young baby you will inevitably have more responsibilities. They will not be able to tell you if they are hungry, tired or in pain and it will be your responsibility to anticipate their needs and act upon them. You will need to be prepared for a number of things when caring for young babies, such as:

- Being aware of health problems which young babies may be prone to such as febrile convulsions, choking, breathing difficulties, colic and nappy rash.
- You will need to devote much more of your time to amusing a young baby, between naps and feeds, as they are unable to entertain themselves in the way toddlers and older children can.
- Baby's routines are a lot less flexible than those for toddlers and older children and you will need to plan carefully often time-consuming things, such as feeds and nappy changes, and incorporate these into your routines.

Although there are many toys and resources available for the amusement and stimulation of babies, such as play gyms and activity tables, these can often be very expensive. Babies can be amused with simple rattles and you may also like to consider making a 'treasure basket'. A treasure basket consists of a container filled with objects made of natural materials which are specially chosen for their interesting shape and texture. To make a treasure basket you will need a suitable container such as a sturdy cardboard box or wicker basket into which you should place around 20 or so objects selected to stimulate the five senses. Items such as a baby mirror, a clean, dry fir cone, an orange, a pumice stone, a wooden clothes peg, a small cloth bag or sock filled with tissue paper, a piece of felt fabric or velvet and a small bunch of keys are all suitable objects which a baby could enjoy exploring safely. While the baby is exploring these items, you should watch from a safe distance but not interact or break the child's concentration.

Caring for school-aged children

Although most childminders care primarily for children aged from birth to five years as this is when the majority of children are requiring day care, they may also agree to take and collect children from school and provide a service caring for school-aged children during the holidays.

If you decide to branch out into caring for school-aged children it is vital that you are aware of their needs and do not expect them to simply fend for themselves while you give your time and attention to the younger children. Only agree to take on the responsibility of caring for school-aged children if you can give them the attention and resources they require.

Things to consider before agreeing to provide care for school-aged children:

1 You will need to fit school drop-off and collections into your daily routine. This is not always easy if you are already caring for a baby who needs regular feeds and naps.
2 You will need to provide extra toys and resources suitable for children aged over five years which, in addition to the toys provided for the younger children, may prove costly.
3 You will need to ensure that you have the space available for the older children to play away from the younger ones.
4 You must understand that the older children will require different things from a childminder than the younger ones. They may not need the help with feeding and toilet training, however, they may need your assistance when completing homework or practicing spellings and you must ensure that the care provided for the older children is not compromised by that given to the younger ones.
5 You may be required to care for the children in the school holidays. While it may be easy for you to provide entertainment for a couple of hours a day in term time, can you reasonably extend this to up to 10 hours per day in the school holidays and, importantly, will the children be happy mixing with babies and toddlers if they are not used to this?

If you care for school-aged children it may often be the case that the parents of these children will only venture into the school on open days and parents' evenings. It is therefore essential that you ensure that you have a good working relationship with both the child's parents and the school. You may need to check whether the school has any letters for the child's parents and, if the parents have a letter for their child's teacher, you will need to ensure that this gets handed in. You may also need to ensure that important things are handed in on time such as completed homework, lunch money, etc. as young children are often forgetful. A three-way method of communication must be sought in order to keep everyone up-to-date.

When deciding on after-school activities for older children it is a good idea to take your cue from the school itself. Ask the children and their teacher what is being taught at the moment and try to work your own activities and themes into the curriculum already in place. This will further enhance the child's learning at school and help to reiterate anything they are unsure of. Remember you will have a lot less time to plan suitable activities for children as the time will be limited to perhaps an hour before school and a couple of hours after school. Some parents may ask you to help their child with their homework and, if the child is happy to do their homework straight from school at your house, then this is all very well. However, it is important to remember that children, particularly those who have just started school, may well be exhausted after a full day at school and are simply not ready to continue learning when they reach their childminder's home. If this is the case, allow them to wind down and spend their time playing, looking at a book or sitting quietly with a drink or a snack. Explain to their parents politely that, while you are willing to help their child with their homework or practise their reading, you are not prepared to force this extra work upon them after they have had a full day at school and you should aim to work out a suitable solution together.

Suitable activities for children after school may include:

Figure 14.3

- Board games
- Card games
- Reading
- Painting
- Drawing and other crafts
- Outdoor play.

The school holidays often provide a good time to embark on activities which may take up more time than is available before and after school, and you could use the holidays to encourage the children to take part in baking and cooking, modelling and sewing, as well as planning suitable trips and outings.

Exercise

Make a list of suitable outings which you could take the children on in the school holidays. Contact your local authority for information about any activities they may provide in your local parks and libraries.

Combining the care of younger children with that of school-aged children

As mentioned previously, when combining the care of school-aged children with younger children, it is paramount that you can provide the attention the school-aged children will require without adversely affecting the care you provide for the younger children. It is also essential that you plan your routines meticulously in order for everything to work successfully and so that the children arrive at, and are collected from school on time. You must not assume that because the school-aged children are older, they will not be as demanding of your time as the younger ones as this is quite simply not the case. Some children of five and six can be equally, if not more, demanding than younger children and if you are caring for the elder sibling of a baby you may find the older child competing for your attention.

Exercise

Think about the problems that you may encounter when caring for school-aged children as well as younger children. How can you ensure that a baby is not disturbed when the older children are making a noise? How can you ensure that the toys allowed are suitable for the ages of all the children you are caring for?

Case Study 14

Jackie cares for two children during the day, one-year-old Catherine and three-year-old Ben. In addition to these younger children Jackie also provides before- and after-school care for Isobel three days per week. Isobel also requires care in the school holidays, whereas Catherine and Ben are the children of school teachers and are not usually with Jackie during school holidays. Isobel, who is 9, has begun to push the boundaries of behaviour and is often rude and disruptive. She refuses to listen to what Jackie has to say and often says she is sick of having to play with babies after school and wants to play with her own friends. This particular afternoon when they arrive back at Jackie's house Isobel asks for the beads out so she can make some jewellery. Jackie explains that this is not possible as both Catherine and Ben are too young to be around this kind of activity and the small beads may pose a threat from choking if either child was to put them in their mouth. Jackie suggests that they get the stickle bricks or Duplo out instead so that all the children can play together, but Isobel is unimpressed and complains that she is never allowed to do anything at Jackie's house and that she is bored and fed up with pleasing babies. She spends the rest of the time at Jackie's in front of the television flicking from station to station and sulking.

1 Do you think Jackie handled this situation well?
2 Do you think Jackie should inform Isobel's parents of the situation?

Although problems can arise when combining the care of school-aged children with that of babies and toddlers, it is important to remember that solutions can be found and caring for mixed-aged groups of children can be very beneficial. Parents often choose childminders as their ideal childcare option because they are providing a home-based setting and family atmosphere and this very much includes the provision of care for children of mixed-age groups. Often children in a nursery are separated from their siblings as under-ones will have special baby rooms and may spend their time away from their older brothers or sisters. Although there may be initial problems with caring for mixed-aged groups of children, the advantages far outweigh any disadvantages and younger children can learn a lot from watching the activities of their peers. All children will benefit from spending time with others of different age groups and will learn how to get along with them and show tolerance and understanding.

Summary

At the end of this chapter you should be able to:

- Identify the different types of play.
- Provide appropriate activities to stimulate young children in the home.
- Explain the advantages of using topics and themes.
- Identify the milestones in a child's development.
- Describe how children can be encouraged to explore their senses.
- Explain the reasons behind the seven Cs and SPICE.
- Describe the Birth to Three Matters framework.
- Summarize the responsibilities involved in caring for babies.
- Identify ways of combining the care of younger children with that of school-aged children.

Useful Websites

www.bakerross.co.uk
   Baker Ross – useful for ordering resources

www.earlyyearsresources.co.uk
   Early Years Resources

www.elc.co.uk
   Early Learning Centre – useful for ordering resources

www.everychildmatters.gov.uk
   Every Child Matters

www.orders@hope-education.co.uk
Hope Education
Tel: 08451 202055

www.scholastic.co.uk
Nursery Education

www.ss-services.co.uk
S & S Services – useful for ordering resources

Managing Children's Behaviour

National Standards
- Standard 3 – Care, Learning and Play
- Standard 9 – Equal Opportunities
- Standard 11 – Behaviour
- Standard 12 – Working in Partnership with Parents and Carers
- Standard 14 – Documentation

Units of the Diploma in Home-based Childcare
- Unit 1 – Introduction to Childcare Practice (Home-based)
- Unit 2 – Childcare and Child Development (0–16) in the Home-based Setting
- Unit 3 – The Childcare Practitioner in the Home-based Setting
- Unit 4 – Working in Partnership with Parents in the Home-based Setting

A framework for dealing with unwanted behaviour

It is important to remember that every family will have a different view on what constitutes acceptable behaviour. Each family will have their own rules and boundaries and all parents will have different expectations of what they expect from their children.

As a childminder you must work with the parents of the children you are caring for in order to find a strategy that is acceptable to everyone. Although families will have their own set of rules for when they are at home, they must also accept that when the children are in your care there may be certain other rules they must abide by in order for everyone to feel welcome and safe. These rules need to be made very clear to both the child and their parents. It is important to remember that children need boundaries in order to feel safe and secure and in order for the child to understand and adhere to your rules they must be clear and consistent.

When deciding on a framework for dealing with unwanted behaviour it is necessary first to look at what constitutes 'unwanted' behaviour.

Exercise

Make a list of the kind of behaviour you would consider to be unacceptable to you.

It is inevitable that the list you make for the above exercise will differ greatly from the next person's. This is because we all have different opinions on what we consider to be acceptable and unacceptable behaviour. For example, you may insist that a child in your care always asks before helping themselves to a drink or snack, whereas at home they may have no such restrictions.

In my own experience one of the most difficult times of the day for establishing boundaries for behaviour is when parents come to collect their child. It seems to me that these are the times when even the best laid plans come unstuck. Children seem to be of the opinion that when a parent is present they are allowed to do whatever they want regardless of whether this is classed as unacceptable behaviour at other times of the day. The reason for this is simple. The child is pushing the boundaries and effectively playing one adult off against the other. When their parents are present they are unsure of who is 'in charge' and whose rules actually apply. It is important that you work with the child's parents in order to eliminate this particular problem as, if the child feels they can push the boundary on one occasion it is inevitable they will attempt to do it regularly. Never be afraid to reiterate a particular rule just because a parent is present. If a child is doing something in front of their parent, which they would not normally be allowed to do, then tell them. You will not do anyone any favours by allowing the child to break your rules and you will actually be giving out confusing messages, particularly if other children are also present.

Case Study 15

Penny is a childminder caring for three children aged between 13 months and three years. Harriet, the oldest child, has begun to run around indoors despite the fact that Penny has clearly pointed out to Harriet that this is not acceptable and could cause an accident. Harriet says she is allowed to run around at home but Penny explains that this does not mean she can do it at Penny's house. She explains that Dominic, who is two years old, will also think he can run around and with two children running someone could get hurt. Despite several reminders throughout the day to stop running, Harriet begins to chase Dominic as soon as her father comes to collect her. Penny reminds Harriet that she is not allowed to run indoors and waits for Harriet's father to back her up. Harriet's father remains silent and Harriet continues to chase Dominic. Penny says nothing else and goes to fetch Harriet's coat. Several minutes later while still being chased by Harriet, Dominic falls and bangs his leg on the table and begins to cry. Harriet promptly puts her coat on and leaves with her father.

1 Do you think Penny handled this situation well?
2 Was Penny being consistent with her boundaries for behaviour, or was she giving mixed messages both to Harriet and the other children?
3 How could this situation be avoided in the future?

Quite often all that is needed to stop a child from crossing the boundaries of unacceptable behaviour in your setting is a polite but firm reminder of your 'house rules'. Every child in your care should be made aware of your rules for behaviour and it is important that they are reminded of what is expected of them from time to time.

Although everyone's opinions of unacceptable behaviour will differ, the list below is perhaps one which should be used as a guide when deciding what to accept or not. Behaviour is unacceptable if:

- It is dangerous either to the child themself or someone else
- It is hurtful or offensive
- It will make the child unwelcome in other people's homes
- It is unacceptable to other people
- It would cause damage to other people's property or possessions.

Factors which influence children's behaviour

There are many factors which may influence a child's behaviour. As behaviour is learnt initially at home it is probably true to say that any immediate changes in a child's home life will have an effect on their behaviour. Not all changes in family circumstances will have a negative affect on a child's behaviour, however, it is worth bearing in mind the following factors when establishing how to manage a child's behaviour:

- The birth of a baby
- The death of a family member or close friend
- Divorce or separation of the child's parents
- Illness within the family
- Abuse or neglect
- Cultural opinions and views
- Moving house
- Unemployment within the family
- Re-marriage of one or both parents
- Death of a pet
- Disability within the family.

Although some of the factors above are more serious than others, it is important to remember that all children will deal with situations differently and while one child may not be too bothered about moving house and see it as a new adventure, another child may be devastated at the prospect of moving away from familiar surroundings and good friends.

Whatever situation a child is experiencing, it is important that you work together with the child's parents to give the child the support they need and to work through any changes as sympathetically as possible.

How to encourage positive behaviour and promote self-worth

Children need to be absorbed in interesting activities which capture their imagination and hold their interest. Once you begin to lose a child's interest they will quickly become bored and start to look for alternative entertainment, often resulting in unacceptable behaviour. It is important for childminders to think carefully about the activities they provide and plan suitable activities at the right level for the child's stage of development. Children should be *actively* involved in activities rather than having to watch an adult in order to keep their interest. It is important for you to be enthusiastic and interested in what the children are doing and give them lots of praise and encouragement when they are showing good behaviour.

In my experience children respond well to praise and encouragement and often like to please the adults they are with. It is your job to build on this and encourage the children to act responsibly towards others and show respect and consideration. Always bear in mind that, although praise is effective, it is important that you do not over praise as it will then become meaningless. Children need to feel good about themselves and it is up to their parents and carers to encourage this by offering praise where it is due and by being good role models. Always make sure that you are fair and consistent and avoid the temptation to give in to tantrums. Offer the children positive choices rather than scolding them. If a child asks to do something inappropriate think carefully about how you refuse their request. Rather than simply saying no try explaining your reasons and offering an alternative.

Exercise

When working with the children take time to consider what you say to them. Make a note of how many times you give *negative* responses to a child's behaviour in the course of a morning and then think about ways you could have been *positive*. For example:

1 Instead of saying 'don't make a mess' try saying 'let's tidy up together'.
2 Instead of saying 'don't tear the pages in that book' try suggesting that you look at the book together or find a more appropriate book suitable to the child's age, such as one with cardboard pages rather than paper.
3 Instead of telling a child to stop running indoors try saying 'it can be dangerous to run inside, why don't we go into the garden if you would like to run around?'.

By thinking about your own responses to a child's behaviour and turning any negative comments or instructions into positive ones you can manage their behaviour effectively without undermining their confidence.

Setting house rules and guidelines for dealing with behaviour

After reading Chapter 9 of this book you should understand the importance of introducing policies to your setting and be confident in writing these. A behaviour policy is essential for all childminders and it is imperative that your setting has a policy for managing behaviour that is suitable for the children you are caring for and this policy must be adhered to at all times in order to provide consistency of care.

Every childminder's house rules will differ depending on their own environment and what is or is not acceptable to them. Your rules must be fair and consistent and most importantly understood by everyone. Your rules should be discussed with both the parents and the children and explanations for the rules should be offered. Try to have as few rules as possible in order that the children can remember them and abide by them. Having four or five important rules which all the children understand and accept is preferable to having a list of 20 which no one can remember and therefore are mainly ignored. You must bear in mind the age and stage of understanding of the children in your care and ensure that you have realistic expectations.

Involving parents in discipline

Parents should always be involved in the discipline of their children. You must discuss your rules and boundaries with the parents and work out a suitable strategy *together*. Remember that it is rewards and punishments which shape a child's behaviour and, in order to avoid confusion, it is absolutely essential that the primary carers in a child's life share the same values and have similar expectations of the child. Children will come from a variety of backgrounds with varying beliefs and expectations and it is not always easy to find a balance to suit everyone. It will be necessary to compromise in some situations and this is why it is important for childminders to discuss their framework for behaviour with the child's parents so that any differences in opinions and ideas can be worked out and suitable strategies found. For example, a parent may believe that the best form of punishment for a child is to sit them on a 'naughty chair'. You may be absolutely appalled by the idea of humiliating a child in this way, however, it is not your place to criticize parenting methods chosen by individuals, although it will be necessary for you to explain why you cannot discipline a child in your own setting in this way. Be careful not to appear to be judgemental but offer alternatives to the parent. They may consider your own methods of responding to unwanted behaviour to be effective and may even try them at home. Primarily you must find your own way of managing children's behaviour in a way that works for you when caring for a number of children of differing ages and from a variety of backgrounds.

Nannies

As nannies work in the children's home there may be times when the parents are present and in these cases you should avoid reprimanding the children or imposing punishments if the parents are clearly in charge of their children at the time. Never interfere with the way a parent deals with a situation involving discipline.

The smacking debate

Childminders must *never* use any type of physical punishment on a child in their care. If you are a member of the National Childminding Association you will have signed up to their Quality Standards which states that childminders must not smack children in their care.

The United Kingdom is one of the last European countries which still allows parents to legally smack their children, despite signing the United Nations Convention on the Rights of the Child over ten years ago.

If you care for a child whose parents use smacking as a method of punishment you may have added problems when it comes to disciplining them yourself. However, with careful thought this problem can be overcome. You are not in a position to use or threaten to use physical punishment but, as an experienced childcarer, you should have the knowledge to enable you to correct unacceptable behaviour in other ways, for example, ignoring a child who is showing signs of unacceptable behaviour and offering praise and rewards to those who are behaving well.

Many people believe that smacking teaches children to become violent themselves and gives the wrong signal that it is acceptable to inflict pain on others. On the other hand some parents believe that a quick smack is an effective way of stopping a child from behaving in a certain way. Again, it is not your job to be judgemental of the ways that parents choose to discipline their children, but you must explain to parents that smacking is not an option for you, as a childminder, and therefore alternative methods of managing behaviour must be sought. *Never* resort to smacking a child, even if their parent has given you permission. It is no longer permitted for childminders to smack the children in their care, even with written parental agreement. As a professional person offering a service of caring for other people's children, there should *never* be a case where you are justified in administering any form of physical punishment and you should use your training and experience to provide suitable ways of managing children's behaviour.

Responding to unwanted behaviour

So how can you punish a child who is showing signs of unwanted behaviour? Firstly, you must look at whether 'punishment' is actually needed. What exactly is the child doing wrong? Are they aware that their behaviour is unacceptable? Sometimes all that is needed is an explanation in order for a child to be aware that what they are doing is not acceptable and this may be the end of the matter. Of course, very young children may need constant reminders as their level of understanding is still low. There may be times however when children who know your rules persistently show signs of unacceptable behaviour and, even after reminding them that what they are doing is unacceptable and offering explanations why, they may ignore you and continue to act badly. This is when you must have strategies in place to deal with unacceptable behaviour. Depending on the nature of the situation, you may like to consider using the following methods of managing unwanted behaviour:

- Focusing on the other children present and praising them for behaving well, while ignoring the child who is showing unacceptable behaviour.
- Distracting the child in order to take their mind off the unacceptable behaviour they are showing and involving them in something more constructive. Remember that boredom can lead to unwanted behaviour and it is up to you to involve the children in interesting and stimulating activities to prevent them from becoming bored.

- Show your disapproval when necessary and make it clear to the child that the behaviour they are showing will not be tolerated. Tell the child why you disapprove of their behaviour.
- Resist arguing with children. You are the person in control of the situation and as such should not need to raise your voice or argue your point. Stay calm in order to remain in control of yourself and the situation.
- Remove the child from the situation. Do not humiliate the child by placing them on a 'naughty chair' or in a 'naughty corner'. It should be sufficient to simply take the child to one side, away from the situation which is causing you concern and give them time to calm down and see the error of their ways. If the child resorts to a tantrum or sulks, allow them to calm down before offering cuddles and reassurance but do not let them take control of the situation to avoid a tantrum.
- Ignore behaviour such as swearing as the attention given or shock shown can often encourage the child to continue saying the words. Remember, children showing this type of unacceptable behaviour are usually seeking attention and *any* kind of attention, even if negative, is better to them than none, therefore do not reward their behaviour by responding to it.

Limit your punishments. Often adults see unacceptable behaviour in many situations when, if thought through, are only situations where children are simply being children. If you dole out harsh punishments for the simplest of misdemeandours you will find it difficult to find appropriate punishments for the more important issues.

If you do consider it necessary to punish a child then do this immediately and make sure that the punishment is appropriate to the child's age and level of understanding. Always forgive and forget after an incident and never drag it on.

Ensure that the child knows that it is their behaviour that is unwanted and not the child themselves.

Nannies

Although it is important to work with the parents of the children you are caring for as much as possible to find suitable strategies for responding to unwanted behaviour, childminders should also bear in mind that, as they will probably be caring for several children from different families, they will have to find solutions which are acceptable to everyone and not simply please one family and expect everyone else to follow suit. In the main, therefore, it will be the responsibility of the childminder to find the best framework for managing children's behaviour, one which suits their particular situation. Nannies on the other hand will have less control over behaviour issues and must take their cue from the child's parents, their employers, and accept their way of dealing with their children's behaviour.

Although children will inevitably misbehave from time to time, it is important to keep things in perspective and, wherever possible, you should try to encourage positive behaviour in the children you are caring for.

- Keep your rules to a minimum. Too many rules will make it difficult for children to focus on the important issues.
- Have realistic expectations of what a child can understand and achieve.
- Be flexible and open to compromises where possible. Allow children to see you admit when you are wrong and show them that you are willing to listen to their wishes, ideas and concerns.
- Allow children some freedom to make their own decisions where possible. They will need to develop their independence and will resent being told what to do all the time. Offer choices where possible.
- Be clear and consistent. Although it is important to be flexible do not change the boundaries or goals you have set simply for a quiet life and to avoid conflict. Stick to your rules and ensure that when you say 'no' you mean 'no' and you are not open to persuasion.
- Stay calm. Never resort to shouting. If you feel the need to shout you have lost control of the situation. Try counting to ten if you feel you are losing control.
- Be positive. Praise children when they have pleased you and reward good behaviour. You may like to adopt a reward system involving stars, tokens or stickers. Try using a good behaviour chart, which can be very effective for younger children who respond well to seeing stickers or ticks on a chart indicating positive behaviour.
- Let the children hear you praising them to their parents. It is important for a child to know that their parents are informed of their positive behaviour and achievements rather than only telling them when they have misbehaved.

Bullying

Bullying can take a number of forms all of which result in the victim suffering from distress and emotional problems. Bullying can include:

- Physical violence
- Name calling
- Teasing
- Refusal to allow a child to join in with games or activities
- Racial remarks
- Abuse.

As a childminder you will become very close to the children in your care and, over time, will be able to spot any changes in their usual behaviour easily. Symptoms shown by a child who is being bullied can take a number of forms but you should be concerned if a child in your care begins to:

- Show signs of not wanting to attend playgroup, nursery or school.
- Complain of feeling unwell to avoid attending playgroup, nursery or school.
- Appear to be distressed or cry a lot for no explicable reason.
- Show signs of aggression or start to turn the situation around and begin to bully the younger children around them.
- Suffer from disturbed nights or nightmares.
- Show signs of being very hungry after school (signs of having missed lunch, perhaps because someone has stolen their lunch money or packed lunch).
- Come home from school with ripped clothes.
- Suffer from unexplained injuries.
- 'Lose' or 'break' personal items.

If you suspect a child in your care is being bullied you must speak to their parents immediately and decide together what can be done. The parents may go into school themselves and talk to the teachers or they may ask you to do this on their behalf. Never ignore any signs of abuse, but bear in mind that, even if the signs are apparent, the child may deny that anything is happening perhaps through fear of repercussions or simply by preferring to avoid drawing attention to the situation. All schools must have a policy in place for dealing with bullying, and childminders have a responsibility to tackle any bullying alongside the school and the child's parents. Always make sure you have the full facts available and involve the appropriate people. Never try to tackle things yourself or take matters into your own hands.

Summary

At the end of this chapter you should be able to:

- Identify a suitable framework for dealing with unwanted behaviour which is appropriate to your own particular setting.
- Give examples of factors which influence children's behaviour.
- Explain how to encourage positive behaviour in children.
- Summarize the reasons why it is important to set rules for dealing with unwanted behaviour.
- Identify the need for involving parents in their child's discipline.
- Analyse the reasons why smacking is not acceptable.
- Identify the signs of bullying.

Useful Websites

www.bullying.co.uk
Anti Bullying Campaign (Tel: 020 7378 1446)

www.bullyonline.org
 Bully OnLine

www.hacsg.org.uk
 Hyperactive Children's Support Group (HACSG)

www.kidscape.org.uk
 Kidscape, 2 Grosvenor Gardens, London SW1W 0DH, Tel: 020 7730 3300

www.nspcc.org.uk
 National Society for the Prevention of Cruelty to Children, Tel: 0808 800 5000

www.parentlineplus.org.uk
 Parent Line, Tel: 0808 800 2222

Useful Advice for Case Studies

The following is my advice on how to deal with the various case studies within this book. While it is important to remember that there is no right or wrong answer to these case studies there are ways to deal with certain situations which will, hopefully, avoid conflict and distress. Often it is not what we say, but how we say it that makes all the difference. The case studies throughout this book have been specially devised to try to take into account as many of the everyday scenarios that most childminders may come across in the course of their work. Anticipating situations, and being aware of how to deal with them, can make all the difference to the smooth running of your business.

Case study 1 (Chapter 1, Page 4)

1 In this situation Angela and Andrew found a solution to their problem by talking about their concerns with each other and working out a suitable compromise.

2 If Angela and Andrew hadn't talked about the situation it could have led to resentment and conflict between Angela and her son. Andrew would have become stressed and anxious and may even have failed his exams due to the lack of quality study time he may have had.

3 Angela and Andrew found a suitable solution to their problem by ensuring that Andrew had his own study space which the childminded children were not allowed to use. If Angela's home had been small and Andrew could not have had his own space then other compromises would have to have been sought. These may have included the following:

- During school holidays Angela could have agreed to take the children out of the house for set periods of time to allow Andrew the space he needed to study. Angela could have arranged a trip to the park or soft-play gym, giving Andrew a whole morning or afternoon to organize his study work.
- Angela could have agreed to give her son the space he needed after the children had gone home or on a weekend by ensuring that he had the house to himself whenever possible in order for him to concentrate on his studies without any distractions.
- Andrew could have made arrangements to study at a friend's house, at the library or on school premises.

Case study 2 (Chapter 3, Page 33)

1 Anne definitely did the correct thing by refusing to begin childminding until her registration had been granted. She would have been breaking the law if she had started to care for a child before her registration had been granted and all the relevant checks made. If she had, she would have risked having her registration refused and may even have been liable to a fine.

2 There are many implications which Anne may have faced if she had begun to childmind before her registration had been granted:
- If the child had been involved in an accident she would not have had the relevant insurance cover in place.
- She may have been reported by someone for childminding without being registered and forced to pay a fine or have her registration refused.
- If she incurred any problems with parents or the child whom she had agreed to care for she would not be able to seek help or advice.
- If word got out that she was working before registration had been granted she could risk her reputation as a professional childminder.

Case study 3 (Chapter 4, Page 52)

1 Anne was right to talk to Adele about her concerns as Adele's persistent lateness was having an effect of Adele's life *outside* her contracted working hours. The fact that Anne was attending an evening class made it more important for her to finish on time. Always remember that when you have set your working hours you are entitled to finish at the agreed time, and should not be expected to work later unless special arrangements have been made.

2 Anne handled the situation very well. There were no arguments or resentment and her request and explanation had the desired outcome.

3 If Adele continued to collect Ben late, or found it difficult to get to Anne's house on time even after trying, Adele could:
- Arrange for someone else to collect Ben on that particular day so that Anne could attend her classes.
- Ask at work about the possibility of leaving 10–15 minutes earlier to avoid the traffic on this particular day if she agreed to make up the time during her lunch break. (Obviously this would depend on the nature of the employment and the flexibility available.)
- Request that Anne drops Ben off at their house on her way to the college. If this arrangement was adopted, a fee should be negotiated for the extra time Anne is caring for Ben and perhaps for petrol expenses if Anne is going out of her way to take Ben home.

Case study 4 (Chapter 5, Page 60)

1 As the children all ended up happy and playing with something which was acceptable to all, Cathy did handle the situation correctly. However, you should bear in mind that not all children will be as accommodating as this and may well feel unhappy having to take a baby's safety into consideration.

2 Cathy must ensure that she offers the children the chance to play with the Lego as soon as the baby is asleep, even if they appear to be engrossed in another activity. The offer may be turned down but it is essential that Cathy keeps her side of the agreement and rewards the children's behaviour for accepting that the Lego posed a risk to the baby.

3 There are of course other ways in which Cathy could have handled this situation and, if the older children hadn't been so accommodating, she may have had to think about an alternative solution such as:

- Requesting that the children play with the Lego on a table out of the baby's reach.
- Requesting that the children play with the Lego in another room. This will depend on the layout of your own home and you should not shut children away to play on their own. However, you may have a dining room, for example, leading from the lounge and, with the use of a safety gate to prevent the baby from entering, the children can still play with the Lego bricks while being in sight and sound of their carer.
- Perhaps, if one was available, the baby could have been put in a playpen for half an hour with some entertaining toys of their own.

Case study 5 (Chapter 5, Page 71)

1 Carole and Alana have been very sensible when working out a solution to this potential problem. They have both identified their own strengths and admitted their weaknesses and, in theory, this situation should work well as both childminders are happy and confident with their defined roles.

2 Problems may occur when one of the childminders is ill. If they are only away from the setting for a short time then things will probably run smoothly, but imagine the problems faced if one of them is away from the setting for several weeks.

3 You may like to consider other solutions if you find yourself in this situation:

- Consider enrolling on a suitable course which will help you to overcome any weaknesses in your childminding abilities. A course involving book keeping and paperwork may well be beneficial for Carol to help her with her lack of knowledge in this area and Alana could look into suitable courses for planning and providing activities for children. Local colleges will have details of courses to assist childminders in all aspects of their job.
- The two could get together periodically and help one another to overcome their problems. Alana could teach Carol about book keeping and Carol could help Alana with decisions about planning activities. The pair could then have 'trial' periods where they swapped roles until each became confident with all aspects of running the business.

Case study 6 (Chapter 6, Page 80)

1 Brenda handled this situation very well. She remained calm and in control of the situation despite the parents allowing their son to jump on her furniture and alter the days they had originally asked for. Brenda was astute and used the interview as a means of deciding whether she could work with the parents and, after concluding that she could not, she did not allow herself to be open to persuasion but suggested that Lena and Bob look elsewhere for suitable childcare.

2 Brenda should have insisted that Lenny stop jumping on her furniture, politely pointing out to Bob that although this may be acceptable at home, it was necessary for her as a childminder to have certain rules in order to protect her own home and ensure the safety of all the children present. She could have shown Bob and Lena a copy of her behaviour policy, while pointing out that jumping on the furniture was one of the things she was not prepared to accept.

3 Brenda could have avoided the problem arising, with regard to the change in days and times requested for childcare by making it clear on the telephone that she was very busy and would not be able to offer flexibility.

Case study 7 (Chapter 7, Page 90)

1 Julie was right to show Susan a copy of the contract and point out that she had agreed its terms when she signed it. She should try not to feel guilty about charging a retainer as she is already taking a substantial loss in earnings by agreeing to charge a reduced fee during all the school holidays. Julie should not consider waiving the retainer fee in order to keep Susan happy if this will mean that her business will suffer as a result.

2 It would have been a good idea if Julie had:
   - Explained to Susan why the retainer had to be charged. Julie should have made it clear that although she was charging a retainer, it was at a substantial reduction in her usual fee and that she was unable to fill Amanda's place during the holidays. She could have pointed out that if she didn't charge a retainer she would be unable to offer Amanda a place as she could not afford to have so many unpaid weeks per annum left vacant.
   - Julie and Susan could have tried to find a compromise, perhaps by Julie agreeing to care for Amanda one or two days per week at the full fee and waiving the retainer for the other days. This way Julie would still be earning a wage and Susan would not feel as if she were paying Julie for 'doing nothing'.
   - Julie could agree to advertise Amanda's place during the holidays and if she found a suitable candidate waive the retainer fees which Susan was paying on the understanding that Amanda would never require childcare during the holidays.

3 This whole situation may have been avoided had Julie ensured that Susan and Geoff completely understood the terms of the contract before they signed. Julie should have explained, in detail, the purpose of the retainer and why it was necessary. If Susan and Geoff were not happy with the arrangement, they should have raised any concerns at contract signing stage rather than later when the placement had begun, making it easier for compromises to be made.

Case study 8 (Chapter 8, Page 106)

1 Jeremy was perfectly right to speak to Lynda and request that she bring a coat for Poppy. It is essential to Poppy's well being that she is provided with clothing appropriate for the weather conditions. Although it is not Jeremy's responsibility to clothe Poppy, it may be helpful if he had a spare coat for situations like this; perhaps an old one which belonged to his own child could be saved in case the need arose again. Jeremy should ensure that his contracts state that it is the parents' responsibility to provide the necessary clothes and equipment needed to adequately care for their children and he should list which items he needs the parents to provide. Jeremy could have reminded Lynda that she had agreed to these terms when she signed the contract.

2 Jeremy needs to find out if there is anything else bothering Lynda and, to avoid Poppy picking up on any anxieties between her childminder and her mother, they need to find a solution to what still appears to be a problem between them. Jeremy could suggest to Lynda that they have a chat, perhaps over coffee, to clear the air. It may be preferable to speak when no children are present and if this is the case a suitable time should be agreed. By sitting down and talking, Jeremy and Lynda should be able to reach a compromise and each will then be aware of how the other is feeling. Communication is absolutely vital if a good working relationship is to be maintained.

Case study 9 (Chapter 9, Page 112)

1 Before agreeing to alter her usual routine to accommodate Natalie's parents' wishes, Georgina should have taken the wishes of all the other parents and children into account. Natalie's parents may well feel that walking to school is more beneficial for their daughter but the parents of one of the other children in Georgina's care may well feel very differently. Georgina needs to consider the wishes of the parents of her present children and, if necessary, seek their opinions before agreeing to change her plans to accommodate a new child.

2 Georgina may well have avoided this situation if she had explained the situation clearly to Natalie's parents in the first instance. She should have pointed out that the 15 minute walk could be made dangerous and unpleasant if the weather was bad or the children had a lot of equipment to carry, such as school bags and lunch boxes. Georgina could have outlined her plans to ensure that Natalie received an adequate amount of daily fresh air and exercise in other ways – perhaps a leisurely walk after lunch or a play in the park.

3 In addition to agreeing to take Natalie out on walks and to the park, Georgina could also seek a compromise to keep everyone happy by promising to use the car only in adverse weather conditions and, when the weather was fine, she could walk the children to school. She should make it clear that this compromise would have to be acceptable to all the parents and that she would still require written permission from them for the times that Natalie would be in the car.

Case study 10 (Chapter 10, Page 120)

1 Yes, Claire did respond to Thomas's symptoms correctly. Having already been warned about the possibility of teething problems, Claire had requested written permission from Thomas' dad to administer the medication he had brought with him that morning.

2 If the medication had not brought Thomas's temperature down Claire should have contacted the child's parents immediately and requested that they collect him with a view to taking him to the doctor. It is important to remember that high temperatures in children that cannot be lowered may lead to convulsions and medical assistance must be sought. While waiting for Thomas's parents to arrive Claire should continue to monitor Thomas, keep the room cool and airy, and remove excess clothing. Sponging with tepid water may also help.

Case study 11 (Chapter 11, Page 134)

1 Anthony could have handled this situation much better. Although he chastised Jade and Ben for laughing at the gentleman, he offered no explanation as to why their behaviour was unacceptable.

2 Jade may have stopped laughing but it is likely she was confused and most certainly would not have understood the consequences of her actions as Anthony clearly failed to explain them.

3 Anthony should have explained to Jade and Ben that the 'bandage' was in fact a turban. He could then have gone on to explain why some men wear turbans. Anthony should have also ensured that Jade and Ben were aware how hurtful laughing at someone can be and that this can cause embarrassment and distress.

4 Anthony could prevent similar occurrences in the future by encouraging the children in his care to ask questions about things they are unsure of or do not understand. Anthony must ensure that he answers questions honestly and in a way that the children will understand.

Case study 12 (Chapter 12, Page 145)

1 Joanne should have sought an explanation from Jasmin's father, Dominic, when he dropped his daughter off that morning. If it was obvious that Jasmin had been crying, and Joanne could have asked why she was upset. Joanne should *not* have prompted Jasmin for an explanation, nor should she have questioned her about the severity of the smack.

2 Although there appears to be no *obvious* reasons for Joanne to assume that Dominic is abusing his daughter, Joanne is jumping to conclusions for a number of reasons:
- Jasmin has told her that her daddy has smacked her.
- Dominic often collects his daughter from Joanne's house late.
- Dominic always appears to be in a rush.

3 These are not valid reasons for suspecting abuse as there is no 'real' evidence. Joanne only has Jasmin's word for what happened that morning and she admits that the children appear to be well cared for in other respects. When Jasmin gets upset she tells Joanne that she wants to go home; this is not something you would expect a child to say if she was unhappy there.

4 Joanne should speak to Dominic. She should arrange a suitable time, when neither is in a rush, and sit down to discuss the present arrangements. It may be that Joanne can help Dominic out by offering longer working hours so that Dominic does not have to constantly rush in order to collect his daughter on time. Joanne could offer to give Jasmin breakfast at her house if this would make mornings easier and less hectic for the family. It is important that Joanne tries to work *with* Dominic and is not seen to criticize his parenting skills. It may simply be that Dominic has a lot of responsibility to shoulder and is still getting over the loss of his wife. Joanne should continue to monitor the situation and make a note of anything which gives her reason for concern.

Case study 13 (Chapter 13, Page 161)

1 Although Victoria did the correct thing by refusing to give in to John's demands to eat the same food as the other children – which would have been going against his parents' wishes of providing a vegetarian diet – she could have handled the situation more effectively by planning her meals in advance and ensuring all the children were offered similar food but in accordance with their dietary practices.

2 Victoria could avoid this situation in the future by planning and preparing meals which could be served to all the children rather than by making individual meals. Children do not like to appear 'different' from their friends and can often get upset if they feel they are the 'odd one out'. Victoria could have overcome this situation by making sure she had some vegetarian sausages to serve to John, so that he could have the same lunch as his friends while sticking to the vegetarian diet his parents have requested. There are many vegetarian alternatives and Victoria needs to plan her menus carefully in order to provide suitable meals for John which will not make him feel 'different' from the other children.

3 Victoria should inform John's parents about the incident for two reasons. Firstly, because John had been upset, and secondly because he had not eaten his lunch that day. Victoria should explain what had happened to John's parents and inform them of her plans to avoid this kind of incident occurring in the future. She should include John's parents in any decisions and ask for their advice.

Case study 14 (Chapter 14, Page 184)

1 Jackie explained the reasons for her decision to Isobel well, however, she could have tried to find a compromise which ensured that *all* the children were happy and safe. It is often difficult to combine suitable activities for school-aged children with those for younger children and it requires careful planning, thought and compromise. On this occasion Jackie could have agreed to Isobel making jewellery provided she did so on the dining room table so that the beads were well away from the younger children. Jackie should make the time to talk to Isobel and explain to her that sometimes compromises have to be made. As Isobel is the only child in Jackie's care in the holidays this would be a good time to make Isobel feel really special and to plan activities and outings that she would really enjoy. This way, although realizing that she may have to compromise slightly during term time, she would be rewarded in the holidays.

2 Jackie should inform Isobel's parents of the incident, mainly because she has already noticed a change in Isobel's behaviour and because the situation does not appear to be improving. If a child's behaviour alters sufficiently to give you cause for concern you should always talk to their parents. It may be a phase they are going through which could be associated with growing up, however, it could also be the result of an underlying problem such as bullying. Jackie needs to discuss what should be done with Isobel's parents and they need to work out a suitable solution together.

Case study 15 (Chapter 15, Page 189)

1 Penny did not handle this situation well. Harriet was allowed to continue running indoors despite being completely aware of Penny's rules and having been told to stop. Penny was not in control of the situation and she did not prevent Harriet from showing unacceptable behaviour.

2 Penny was definitely not being consistent with her boundaries and was giving very mixed messages to all the children present. She was allowing Harriet to do something which would not normally be acceptable simply because her father was present.

3 To avoid a similar situation in the future Penny could do a number of things:

- She could talk to Harriet's parents and point out that running indoors was dangerous and not acceptable. She should remind them of her behaviour policy and explain that Harriet was perfectly aware of the rules and, until a parent is present, is usually very good at abiding by them. Penny needs to ask Harriet's parents to support her on this matter in the future.
- Penny should explain the consequences of Harriet's actions to her and point out that her refusal to stop running resulted in Dominic falling and hurting himself, something that Penny had warned Harriet may happen.
- In the unlikely event that a parent refuses to back you up in this kind of situation you should consider removing the temptation. In this kind of situation Penny could ensure that both Harriet and Dominic were engrossed in a quiet activity which required them to be seated when home time was nearing, for example, reading a story or doing a jigsaw.

List of Useful Addresses and Websites

British Allergy Association
Deepdene House
30 Bellgrove Road
Welling
Kent
DA16 3PY
Telephone: 0208 303 8525
Website: www.allergyfoundation.com

British Nutrition Foundation (BNF)
High Holborn House
52–54 High Holborn
London
WC1V 6RQ
Telephone: 020 7404 6504
Website: www.nutrition.org.uk

British Red Cross Society
Westminster Tower
3 Albert Embankment
London
SE1 7SX
Telephone: 0207 388 8777
Website: www.redcross.org.uk

Care Standards Inspectorate for Wales (CSIW)
National Assembly for Wales
Cardiff Bay
Cardiff
CF99 1NA
Telephone: 02920 825111
Website: www.csiw.wales.gov.uk

Child Accident Prevention Trust (CAPT)
Clerks Court
18/20 Farringdon Lane
London
EC1R 3AU
Telephone: 0207 608 3828
Website: www.capt.org.uk

Childcare Link
Telephone: 0800 960 296
Website: www.childcarelink.gov.uk

Commission for Racial Equality
Elliot House
10–12 Allington Street
London
SW1E 5EH
Telephone: 0207 828 7022
Website: www.cre.gov.uk

Council for Awards in Children's Care and Education (CACHE)
8 Chequer Street
St Albans
Hertfordshire
AL1 3XZ
Telephone: 01727 847 636
Website: www.cache.org.uk
E-mail: info@cache.org.uk

Council for Disabled Children
8 Wakely Street
London
EC1V 7QE
Telephone: 0207 843 6000

Department for Education and Skills (DfES)
Telephone: 0870 000 2288
Website: www.dfes.gov.uk
E-mail: info@dfes.gov.uk

Equal Opportunities Commission
Arndale House
Arndale Centre
Manchester
M4 3EQ
Telephone: 0845 601 5901
Website: www.eoc.org.uk
E-mail: info@eoc.org.uk

ICS Distance Learning College
Telephone: 0800 056 3983
Website: www.icslearn.co.uk

Inland Revenue
Telephone: 0845 609 5000 (The helpline for
Working Families Tax Credit)
Website: www.inlandrevenue.gov.uk

Kidscape
2 Grosvenor Gardens
London
SW1W 0DH
Telephone: 0207 730 3300
Website: www.kidscape.org.uk

National Association for Toy and Leisure
Libraries
68 Churchway
London
NW1 1LT
Telephone: 020 7387 9592
Website: www.natll.org.uk
E-mail: admin@natll.ukf.net

National Childminding Association (NCMA)
81 Tweedy Road
Bromley
Kent
BR1 1TW
Telephone: 0845 880 0044
Website: www.ncma.org.uk
E-mail: info@ncma.org.uk

National Extension College
Michael Young Centre
Purbeck Road
Cambridge
CB2 2HN
Telephone: 01223 400350
Website: www.nec.ac.uk/courses

National Society for the Prevention of Cruelty to
Children (NSPCC)
National Centre
42 Curtain Road
London
EC2A 3NH
Telephone: 0207 825 2500
Helpline: 0800 800 5000
Website: www.nspcc.org.uk

Northern Ireland Childminding Association
(NICMA)
Telephone: 0289 181 1015
Website: www.nicma.org

Office for Standards in Education (Ofsted)
Alexandra House
33 Kingsway
London
WC2B 6SE
Telephone: 020 7421 6800
Website: www.ofsted.gov.uk

Parentline plus
520 Highgate Studios
53–79 Highgate Road
Kentish Town
London
NW5 1TL
Telephone: 0207 284 5500
Website: www.parentlineplus.org.uk

Royal Society for the Prevention of Accidents
(RoSPA)
Edgbaston Park
353 Bristol Road
Edgbaston
Birmingham
B5 7ST
Telephone: 0121 248 2000
Website: www.rospa.co.uk
E-mail: help@rospa.co.uk

Scottish Childminding Association (SCMA)
Telephone: 01786 445377
Website: www.childminding.org

Scottish Commission for the Regulation of Care
The Care Commission
Compass House
11 Riverside Drive
Dundee
DD1 4NY
Telephone: 01382 207100
Website: www.carecommission.com

Vegetarian Society
Parkdale
Dunham Road
Altrincham
Cheshire
WA14 4QG
Telephone: 0161 925 2000
Website: www.vegsoc.org.uk

Welfare Food Reimbursement Unit
PO Box 31040
London
SW1V 2FB
Telephone: 020 7887 1212

Index of the National Standards for Childminding

Index of the Diploma of Home-Based Childcare Units

Index